500
WAYS TO
GRADUATE IN
SUCCESSFUL
SELLING

500
WAYS TO
GRADUATE IN
SUCCESSFUL
SELLING

RAJESH KADAM

PARTRIDGE
A Penguin Random House Company

Cover page designed by Milind (milindideas@gmail.com)

To order additional copies of this book, contact
Partridge India
000 800 10062 62
orders.india@partridgepublishing.com

www.partridgepublishing.com/india

Selling is not a rocket science,
everyone can learn it.

—Rajesh Kadam

About the author

The author started his career in a small firm in Mumbai while completing his studies. Hard work and focus is what he believed in and within short time he was serving a MNC at a senior level. At the age of 36, he left the industry to spend quality time with his family.

Acknowledgement

Thanks to all the people who have directly or indirectly contributed in creation of this special book.

Thanks to my beloved wife Rashmi for motivating and supporting me, and my parents, they inspired me a lot through their very existence, and especially to my 2 naughty kids Kunal and Kimaya, who never disturbed me while writing.

Special thanks to my friend and business partner, Indrajeet Rane, who gave a lot of input in bringing the final materialization of this book.

Disclaimer

All the copyrights of this book reside with Mr. Rajesh B. Kadam

Mr. Rajesh B. Kadam shall not be liable or responsible for direct, indirect, incidental or consequential damages if this book is used other than as a reference.

Mr. Rajesh B. Kadam assumes no responsibility and would not be held liable for any misquote or distortion of the contents.

The sole purpose of this book is to inspire individuals to reach their optimal potential as a human and should only be used for the same.

A word to my valued readers

The sole purpose of this book is to explore 500 ways which will add to your success in selling, and to encourage and motivate all sales people in achieving high success in selling, irrespective of what they sale.

Each page is divided into 3 sections—header, body and footer. The header is the topic of discussion. The body is the explanation of the topic. And footer is the extract to remember from the discussion.

Some of the ways discussed in this book will seem familiar and are indeed vastly used in practice in the whole world. This is because; they are into existence since ages. Smart and successful sales professionals have been using these since many years. Most ways covered are of common-sense and professional approach towards sales with basic etiquettes.

This book is written in simple and easy to understand English. The best part of this book is that you can start reading it from any page.

Dedicated to . . .

All the Future Star Sales People

This book is dedicated to all the people who are in sales or willing to start their career in sales to benefit others and to all those who wish to graduate in successful selling.

You will learn good expertise to gain confidence in successful selling, regardless of what product/service you sell.

If any of these 500 ways lead you to new heights of achievement, then this book will have achieved it's purpose.

Thank you for purchasing this book. And please do share your experience at **rajeshbkadam@gmail.com**.

Good Luck and Happy Graduation . . .

Index

26. Convey / convince
27. Do not leave anything for tomorrow
28. Stop controlling customers
29. Keep your workforce happy
30. Self-discipline
31. Follow FIFO method for products
32. People notice how they are treated
33. Create a desire of ownership in customers mind
34. Do not give excuses
35. Never ever bad mouth your competitor
36. Eco friendly things
37. Dress up for calls just as meetings
38. Avoid hangovers of elephant sales
39. Send editorials that benefit customers
40. If you think something is wrong, then something is wrong
41. Sell yourself
42. All customers are important
43. Learn from others mistakes
44. Make it hard for customer to leave you
45. You can make things happen
46. Hire the people you need
47. Interview current clients
48. Sell only one thing at a time
49. People may treat you rudely
50. Take Token payment
51. Do not interrupt
52. Look for repeat-business
53. Your time is the most valuable commodity you have
54. When in doubt, hold back your actions
55. Recognize new trends of your industry

56. Do not ever think that you have no competitors
57. Ask for the Order
58. Hunt for bulk orders
59. Make customers feel great
60. Advertising your product properly
61. Meet decision makers
62. Keep your desk / office clean
63. Handling Mistakes
64. Use emails but don't lose personal touch
65. Make meetings interactive
66. Multi-tasking
67. Keep trying
68. Do not count notional profits
69. Change for positive growth
70. Cultivate a pleasant tone
71. Requisites for a star sales performer
72. Whats IN
73. Whats OUT
74. Keep learning new strategies
75. Use customers' name in discussions
76. Do not drop in without an appointment
77. Sell benefits
78. Demo means educating customer
79. There are no shortcuts
80. Be one step ahead of customer
81. Invest in quality business cards
82. Easy sales / hard sales
83. Your excitement and enthusiasm = your sales
84. You are in REJECTION business
85. Make relationship, not sale

86. Be honest
87. People buy when they are ready to buy
88. Emotional sales
89. Take Responsibility
90. Use words ending with ER-EL-EST
91. There is always a next time
92. Congratulating customers
93. Remember names
94. Meet at customers' convenience
95. Associate with good people
96. Watch audio/video of successful businessmen
97. Essentials of a feedback form
98. What more can you do?
99. Do not repeat call instantly
100. Write down point's immidietly after call / meeting
101. So what if people call u a day dreamer?
102. If you fail to plan, then you are planning to fail
103. Wear a smile
104. Doubt the person who buys without any objection & negotiation
105. Read books of selling/marketing guru's
106. Take a long term view
107. Nobody will believe, until you believe
108. Confirm appointment before going
109. These actions disturb
110. It's not what you have; it's what people think you have
111. To improve, learn to acknowledge your mistakes
112. Add your personal guarantee
113. Rehearse for presentations
114. Do not start with the price first
115. Bad experiences are necessary for your growth

116. High clicked websites
117. I CAN . . . . these 2 words are very important
118. Do not drink, smoke or gamble
119. Feel good factor is essential
120. Selling is getting connected with people
121. When to let go a prospective
122. Your sales funnel should always be full
123. Be ambitious
124. Make as many as good friends as you can
125. Leave your bad attitude
126. Do not allow people to waste your time
127. Always carry a note pad and Pen / pencil with you
128. People do not want cheap product
129. Customers rate TRUST as no.1 requirement
130. Do not discuss your business plans with everyone
131. Closing questions
132. Do not see your product as a commodity
133. Do not be afraid to try new idea
134. Needy people
135. Focus on your target
136. Good relationship = good sales
137. Plan multiple appointments in same territory
138. Keep a good balance of deals
139. Practice self-praise method before going for meeting
140. Awareness vs. sales
141. Study customer / company profile in advance
142. Work ethically
143. If appropriate, share your home contact number
144. It should be a conversation
145. Answer calls within 3-4 rings

146. Do not ever do sympathy sales
147. Always reach 10 to 15 minutes before time
148. Always lead the discussion positively
149. Always carry your business card
150. Old enquiry list
151. Do not interrogate, just ask questions to client
152. Sponsor events for social cause
153. Call @ right time
154. Do not give too much time to a single customer
155. Convince people that you have the best
156. Do not be single tracked for big sale
157. What triggers window shopping
158. Approach your friends and relatives when new in business
159. Do not pre-judge any customers by their appearance
160. Difference between bargaining and negotiation
161. Do not give false promises to customers
162. The person who asks price first, will not buy
163. A "NO" should never demoralize you
164. Copy customers' postures and words
165. You never get a 2nd chance for your 1st impression
166. Give feedback to referrers
167. Be an active listener
168. Do not repeat topic, unless asked
169. Taking feedback is major key point for future sales
170. Do not get tired and give up too soon
171. Identify the right people fit for your product or services
172. Success breeds success
173. Sincerity and Integrity has a very big impact on your sales
174. Sale Statistics
175. Make cold calls to people who did not buy from you

176. Match the talking speed of customer
177. Study your competitors' products / services too
178. Customer who does not store your details . . .
179. Move step by step towards closing the deal
180. Hand gestures
181. Think solutions and not problems
182. Exchange as many as business cards as you can
183. Identify the need of customer
184. Care for customers for autopilot of business
185. You need full confidence in yourself and your product
186. Backup plan
187. Always listen to prospective customer first
188. Give opportunity whenever appropriate
189. Worth of your product / service should be more than the price
190. Show interest in customers' discussion
191. Explain each benefit one by one
192. Accept suggestions, if better than yours
193. Say thanks to people who did not buy from you
194. Do not hold the line
195. Think as if you are self-employed
196. See objections as opportunity
197. Stay in touch with customers
198. Carry competitors' data with you
199. Control yourself
200. Explain fine prints
201. A customer never buys a product
202. Look for a buoyant market
203. Document in black and white
204. Do not give unsolicited advice
205. DND

236. Prioritize customers

237. Only sell your product/service, all the time

238. Clarify questions / objections / doubts

239. Some common terms used in sales

240. Become a sales magnet

241. Think you are the first sales person meeting them

242. Do not take impulsive decisions

243. Make people say "Yes" in conversations

244. Transparency is important

245. Understand the difference between COST and PRICE

246. Do not sound fake on calls

247. Take the challenging path, you may strike gold

248. Offer less choice

249. Use presentation materials only for support

250. Speak to customers just as you speak with family and friends

251. Do not use customers in example

252. Know when to be silent

253. Selling in exhibitions and alike

254. Never use these statements

255. Pearls of wisdom

256. Do not mention designation on business card

257. Prepare for every sales call

258. Go prepared . . . . make a checklist

259. Scrutinize unusual order

260. Suspect and Prospect

261. Get emotionally connected

262. Thoughtful recommendations

263. Think from the goal

264. Remember your bad sales

265. Leave extra order forms / broucher / leaflets

266. Be a positive thinker
267. Dress/ talk in accordance of region
268. What drives sales?
269. Do not discuss your product / service in detail over the phone
270. Ask for testimonial letter from satisfied customers
271. Conversion ratio
272. SWOT Analysis
273. Do not give up follow ups
274. Write down points in meeting
275. Make a list of benefits of your product/service
276. Conclude call/meeting on good note
277. Repeat what works
278. Barter game
279. Discounts and concessions harmful in sales
280. Make eye contacts
281. Think about next 5 sales
282. Never regret
283. Take help from others
284. Attempt trial close
285. Backup important data
286. Set high standards for yourself
287. Selling is caring
288. Do not fix first meeting in hotel/restaurant
289. After sales service
290. Cross sale your products/services immediately
291. What influences buying?
292. 1st objection is mostly a false objection
293. Do not criticize or complain
294. Leave an order form
295. When self-doubt creeps in your mind

296. Quick sales rarely happen
297. Handle all types of customers
298. Join some social club
299. Ask for only 2 referrals at a time
300. Use good quality sales material for presentation
301. Answer all calls with enthusiasm / excitement
302. Be focused on buyers, and not on money
303. Seasonal businesses needs special planning
304. Give options for meeting
305. Word of mouth works the best
306. Create a need for your product/service
307. Give special attention to big / corporate customers
308. Be Positive in your thoughts and deals
309. Appreciate every single person involved with you
310. Become good observer
311. When customers have price objection
312. Do not expect customer to fill forms
313. Your y-o-y growth should be more than market growth
314. Make customer a family
315. Intuitions are bigger than your beliefs
316. Sales is a 24 hour business
317. Learn 5 new words everyday
318. Do not push your business card
319. Believe in yourself and your skills
320. Visit expos to upgrade yourself
321. Pricing with 9
322. Spending habit of a customer
323. Fear of rejection
324. Learn from every sales call / meeting
325. Some people only assure buying, but never buy

326. These things will hold you back

327. These things will support you

328. Make others feel important and significant

329. Utilize everything available

330. You will always find a few unhappy customers

331. Email promotions

332. Keep good relations with influential people

333. Attend complaints yourself (If any)

334. You do not sell, you help in buying

335. Voice mail box

336. Study your previous customers closing timeline

337. Speaker phone

338. Keep asking questions until you get answers

339. Allocate time wisely between customers

340. Do not start selling as soon as you meet

341. Fake it till you make it

342. Give non-precious gifts

343. Do not depend on email and text messages

344. Your personality will help you for first few minutes

345. Prequalified products

346. Do not say "you cannot buy this"

347. Recession

348. Locked up situation

349. Price doesn't matter, but your selling skill does

350. Improve your performance sale after sale

351. Go for training atleast once a year

352. Entertain clients for reasonable time

353. Giving too much information is unhealthy

354. Do not talk too much

355. Delegate your non-essential work to someone

356. Higher price tag next to your product display
357. Reach 5-10 minutes before time
358. Take your colleague with you when meeting big customers
359. Be plural
360. Wear dark suits for meetings
361. Always be optimistic
362. Do not argue with your customer
363. Understand difference between Hearing and Listening
364. Come out of your comfort zone
365. Narrate stories
366. Keep customers hooked up
367. Customer service
368. Some common buying signals
369. Do what you are afraid of doing
370. Blame yourself for failure
371. When new business, protect the downside
372. Take your colleague with you
373. Get along with everyone
374. Be serious with sales, all the time
375. Keep a log of people who did not buy from you
376. Qualities of an unsuccessful salesperson
377. Understand buying motive of customers
378. Stick to your commitments
379. Avoid people who doubt your goals / targets
380. A thing becomes necessity, when your neighbour has it
381. Create a structure for loyal customers
382. Middle price sales
383. Type of questions customer ask
384. When you get a 'YES', take order immidietly
385. Know your competitor

386. Be a 'how' thinker and not 'if' thinker
387. Emotion + Logic = Deal
388. Complete all tasks
389. Study competitors' weaknesses and strengths
390. Appoint informal helpers/associates
391. Share bad news too
392. Customer is NOT always right
393. Work for more than 8 hours a day
394. Follow deadlines
395. Sales doesn't happen by chance, it needs to be planned
396. Be active while presenting
397. Promise less, deliver more
398. Get yourself known as a result-oriented sales person
399. Always ask yourself these questions . . .
400. Do not address customers by their first name
401. Create a network of networks
402. Email or text message after call / meeting
403. Change your presentation according to customers
404. Be ambitious in whatever you do
405. Give only the information which is necessary for a sale
406. Gut feeling
407. Find strong reasons why customer should buy from you
408. Features Vs Benefits
409. When customer abandon online purchase
410. If you are not consistent, then you are moving backwards
411. See new customer as soon as possible
412. Who is prospect?
413. Can you help me out?
414. Thanking for everything
415. People who buy only by price are not loyal customers

446. Quotations

447. Always remember the old 80:20 rule, it still works

448. Immediately apply whatever you have learnt new

449. Don't leave before asking for next appointment

450. You are accountable for everything

451. Umbrella questions

452. Do not put limitations on your ideas

453. Open / close ended questions

454. There are always some common objections

455. Hire cautiously, but fire immediately

456. Do not spend too much time with a customer

457. Never assume clients reactions

458. Respect Law

459. Be alone for 2-3 hours in a week

460. Pricing of your product / services

461. Discount or Extra?

462. Optimism and realism

463. Smart buyers rely on customer reviews

464. Recognize your weaknesses

465. The power of persuasion

466. Everyone gets 24 hours a day

467. Pillar

468. Formal & casual wear

469. Selling is not talking

470. Remember, you are dependent on customer

471. Trust your product/service

472. Most customers do not complain

473. Give sufficient time to decide

474. Leave a good impression everywhere you go

475. Variety of customers

Welcome

Everyone is into sales since birth.

A child asking for chocolates and toys from his/her parents is also doing a type of sales to fulfill his requirements.

A student giving clarifications to a teacher for not completing the homework is also selling his/her reasons to convince them.

Dating also involves selling of love-filled heart and promises of togetherness.

A lone old person wanting to stay with his son, daughter-in-law and grand children is also selling his desire to end his loneliness and wanting attention for his care.

So, we all are sellers since birth . . . . aren't we?

—Rajesh B. Kadam
Author

Qualities of a successful Salesperson

These are a few qualities you will find in a successful salesperson:

- Always smiles
- Shows confidence
- Eager to help others
- Solve problems
- They encourage others
- They show enthusiasm
- Deliver on time
- They do not leave customer until they hear YES or NO.
- Are honest and ethical

Result oriented

Way no. 1 to successful selling

Assure customer that you are just there to help them

Engrave these lines into your mind that you are there to help the customer as a friend in choosing what they are looking for.

You are not a sales person at all; you are a friend, guide, well-wisher, etc for the customer.

Make them realize that, it hardly matters to you if they buy or do not buy from you. You will continue being helpful and caring for them.

This will create a special place for you in their hearts, and you will be looked upon as a friend, thereafter.

Become friend, not a sales person

Way no. 2 to successful selling

Follow a mentor

Everyone needs to follow a mentor to be successful. Be it being in education, business, relations, sales . . . a mentor is a must. You can have more than one mentor.

A mentor effectively tunes his Mentee with authenticity & engages them to achieve the desired goal. They guide them by building trust & sharing positive behaviors.

It's an old saying . . . . If you want to achieve something, you need to follow someone who has already achieved it.

Always follow star sales persons' strategies, methods, thinking, behavior, way of handling different situations, etc., if you wish to be a star sales person.

Teachers also have teachers

Way no. 3 to successful selling

Love your work of sales

Love your sales work and you will never feel you are working. When you enjoy something and love the same, it becomes a passion.

Do not do sales for money, do sales for your passion and your passion will bring you money.

When you do things which you are passionate about, you master them. If you master sales, you become best sales person.

A best sales person is always rewarded with the best benefits.

Sales is victorious

Way no. 4 to successful selling

Write down your goals

You need to plan your goals in advance.

Start with weekly goals, then monthly and then yearly.

Further, sub-divide your goals into days.

Goals can be set in terms of achievements/targets. Work on one goal at a time, this will fuel your thought process & planning.

But first thing is to get into the habit of writing them down, so it is always in front of you and you can figure out where you are falling behind or you have achieved the goal well in advance.

Achievement of one goal is the start of another goal. It's a never ending process.

Writing goals leads to achievements

Way no. 5 to successful selling

Do not outsmart your customer

At times sales people try to beat a customer in debate, this is very unprofessional and shows your arrogance in approach. It needs to be avoided as it may lead to conflict and definitely not help you in sales.

See your customers as friends with whom you wish to associate in business rather than taking them as challengers.

Instead of being outsmart with your customer, try to create a win-win situation where the opportunity of customer satisfaction increases.

Be a friend

Way no. 6 to successful selling

Do not sit in reception area

Never sit in reception area of your customers' office.

Sitting and waiting for someone really builds unnecessary tension in mind.

Instead, just pick up some magazine or stand near window. Or make some calls with controlled voice by standing or slowly moving around the lobby.

If, the reception is small to move around and there is no option other than sitting, then just take out your notebook and go through its pages, surely you will find something to think and plan upon.

The idea is to keep your enthusiasm and motivation fully charged for the meeting.

Be up

Way no. 7 to successful selling

Keep your self-respect

Whatever conditions/situations you are in, but do not ever beg for sales.

You may be in worse situation, you may not have achieved good sales figure, you may have personal or family problems, but how does that matter to customer?

At the most you will get a few sympathy sales, that's it. You will never get more business from these customers again.

Do not beg for sales

Way no. 8 to successful selling

Constructive criticism is for your benefit

It is very difficult to except criticism but accepting criticism in a constructive manner is advisable as it leads to improvement in your abilities.

Accept criticism positively from:
- Family and friends
- High profile personalities
- Knowledgeable people
- Existing customers

Constructive criticism helps you in:
- Knowing your drawbacks and shortfalls
- Learning
- Positive improvements
- Adds value to product
- Make criticizer feel imperative
- Opportunity to succeed

Accept constructive criticism

Way no. 9 to successful selling

Mere degree / certification does not guarantee success in selling

It is a misconception of many individuals that once they have achieved a particular degree / certification, they expect guaranteed success in their respective career.

Degree and certification is a must, but one needs to understand that practical implementation of the theoretical knowledge received is important.

Example:
Winning a war game on some video console does not prepare you to fight the battle in real.

Success = Theory + Practical's

Way no. 10 to successful selling

Try not to sit opposite
to customer

If there is place to sit next to your customer, do occupy the seat as it gives confidence and people take you as a friend rather than sales person.

Some sort of natural bonding comes in existence while talking with someone sitting next to him / her, than sitting opposite.

Agreed the fact that sitting opposite seems more professional but connecting emotionally helps a lot in sales business.

Convincing someone sitting opposite is much difficult than convincing someone sitting next to him / her.

Sit next to customer

Way no. 11 to successful selling

Estimates

Estimates are customer specific and the next level in sales process. It has all details about the product / service with its actual purchasing price finalized after negotiations with the customers.

It may be in full payment or in installments. Your estimation includes all specifications of the actual product / services bought by your customer and its entire payment schedule with dates and mode of payments. A smallest mistake while preparing estimation will definitely be hazardous.

Prepare estimations carefully

Way no. 12 to successful selling

Do not sit between 2 people for explanation

If you are visiting somebody for sales and there are more than one member who wants to get involved with you in decision making process, then sit opposite to the members.

This way you are in better position to explain, as everyone is sitting in front of you, and grasps whatever you say.

Even if there are only 2 people showing interest, still do not sit in between them.

Many times we think sitting in between will be of more help, but it actually does not. You can explain to both, but those 2 people cannot interact amongst each other to discuss or decide anything.

Position yourself

Way no. 13 to successful selling

Inbound / outbound sales

<u>Inbound sales:</u>
It is a lead generated through marketing and advertising strategies. Customers get attracted by the promotions made and approach you, and then the sales are dependent on your selling skills. Chances of conversion are high as the customer is walking upto you.

<u>Outbound sales:</u>
It is also termed as external sale which is related to approaching customers recommended through references, database, etc. Such sales are made by walking upto customers. These customers may not necessarily buy from you. These are hit-or-miss type sales.

Practice both

Way no. 14 to successful selling

Keep audio books

Instead of just travelling, get into habit of listening to sales related motivating and inspiring audio books while on move.

Generally all people travel 1-3 hours daily.
So utilize these hours by feeding your mind with knowledge which will sharpen your skills and performance.

It sounds more personalized as you get a feel that someone is narrating for you. You get more involved when you listen and grasp the content quickly.

Note: NOT RECOMEMNDED WHILE DRIVING

Easy to understand

Way no. 15 to successful selling

Unhappy customer will give you the best input

These are the best people who share the actual drawbacks of your products / services and they are / can be actively involved in improving the products / services.

Example:
A flat owner is not happy with the developer, as he has kept a dumping space in a corner of the premises. Unhappy with the open dumping area, the resident personally develops it into a beautiful garden, and is appreciated by the developer and members of the society.

Best feedbacks

Way no. 16 to successful selling

Keep clients updated with your new product/service

It is a very healthy practice to make your existing customer aware of new products/services as it not only helps your business to grow but also adds value to the relationship with your customer.

Customers feel privileged that you considered them for your new product/service. This indeed helps creating brand loyalty & expansion of business.

It takes fewer efforts to get the optimum response for the new product/ service launched because existing customers have faith in you & also share genuine feed back with their suggestions which help us in improvising the quality of our product / service.

It is utterly important to consult with your existing customers as they are the end-users who have experienced advantages & disadvantages of your products/services.

Brings repeated business

Way no. 17 to successful selling

Non-buyers reference rarely buys

It rarely happens that a reference of a non-buyer will buy from you.

It's natural that, if a customer himself / herself has not bought from you, then they are in no position to convince their friends/relatives to buy.

Following such customers is waste of time and should not be practiced. Giving a try when you are relatively idle is okay.

Follow wisely

Way no. 18 to successful selling

Use sentence like . . .

Including your client while framing sentences really helps.

Example 1

<u>Do not ever say</u>—let me see, what can I do about this?
<u>Instead say</u>—let **us** work out on this, and surely **we** will come out with something, and **our** relation starts.

Example 2

<u>Do not say</u>—let me finish my presentation and then I will discuss things with you.
<u>Instead say</u>—Sir, let **us** first understand the product/services and then **we** can discuss all the doubts **you** have.

Use togetherness in words

Way no. 19 to successful selling

Body language of a buyer

Foot: the foot is pointed towards product or the person the customer has in mind.

Chin stroking: about to take decision.

Upward palm: he is honest and expects the same.

Smile: welcoming attitude and open to hear you.

Open arms: trust me.

Gazing or leaning forward: showing interest in product / service.

Nodding head: in agreement.

Understand and approach accordingly

Way no. 20 to successful selling

Body language of a non-buyer

Crossed arms: offensive signal and is a barrier.

Scratching neck: doubting signal

Scratching nose: the customer is lying or not trusting you.

Scratching head: uncertainty.

Hands in pocket: Does not wish to talk.

Pointing finger: negativity in discussion.

Tight lipped smile: Not willing to share anything with you.

Rubbing eyes or grabbing ear: not interested in your presentation.

Understand and approach accordingly

Way no. 21 to successful selling

Get customers' attention / interest in first 4-5 minutes

Try to win your customers interest / attention in you and your product/ service in first 4-5 minutes as this will increase chances of winning the customers confidence to buy from you and bring you more closer to the deal.

Proper greetings, friendly gestures, presentation manner, maintaining professionalism, etc are few aspects that can catch your customer's attention and win his interest in early minutes.

Attention + interest = Sales

Way no. 22 to successful selling

Make 'tomorrows' task list

Fall in a habit of making a list of next day's tasks as soon as you finish your day.

When your next day's task list is ready before going to bed, you already have plans going on in your sub-conscious mind for the next day.

This task list will help you in visualizing . . .

- What is going to happen tomorrow?
- Where are you going?
- What will you discuss and with whom?
- How will you handle the situation?

Planning in advance saves a lot of time.

Be prepared

Way no. 23 to successful selling

You buy and experience, then sell

Merely reading your brochures and going through trainings will not be helpful in sales. To get a real feel for representing your product / service, you need to experience it first. Your experience will add value in your presentations. Understanding towards your product / service becomes clearer when you practically use them.

You become aware of limitations, drawbacks, negative aspects of product / service after your experience, which prepare you to wisely handle objections raised by your customers.

Learn and earn

Way no. 24 to successful selling

Demonstrate your product/service

Demonstration of your product/service will create buying interest in persons mind.

Demonstrate it in such a way that people link its necessity with their needs.

Make them realize how it will save their time and money.

Customers get to study the actual working of the product/service. Such operation helps in clear understanding and avoids errors/accidents that can happen if not demonstrated by a trained professional.

Demonstration makes the customer more bias for your product/service.

Demonstrate

Way no. 25 to successful selling

Convey / convince

It will be a mistake if you try to convince prior to conveying the benefits of your product / service. Also, merely conveying your message is just not going to be fruitful to you without convincing your customer.

Sales professionals should always be focused on convincing their customers for buying their products / services rather than just conveying.

Conveying is not a tool in sales.

Conveying never brings business

Way no. 26 to successful selling

Do not leave anything for tomorrow

If you can't do it today, what different and special are you expecting about tomorrow?

Tomorrow will also be the same 24 hours.

Since, there is nothing special about tomorrow, so do it today, everything you wish to do.

If you can't do today, probably you can't do it tomorrow too, and thus, the work gets delayed and never done.

You will get thousands reasons for not doing it today.
You just need to find that one good reason to do it today.

Tomorrow never comes.

Avoid Procrastination

Way no. 27 to successful selling

Stop controlling customers

We all hate being controlled by anyone, especially if they are strangers like salespeople. You are approaching them at their will and entering their personal periphery. Stop controlling the customer, and he / she will start to cooperate with you.

People buy from those who do not interfere or try to control them. To gain the reputation you need to let them have their own space and allow them to express themselves first.

Control yourself

Way no. 28 to successful selling

Keep your workforce happy

Establish a healthy working environment amongst your team members. It maintains favorable conditions to excel and perform consistently.

A delighted team benefits in several ways:

- Always high spirited
- Result oriented performance
- Ready to deliver extra
- Organizations branding
- Good bonding and responsible attitude
- Authority
- Creativity in work
- Serve you for long term
- Loyalty
- Growth opportunities
- Hustle free operations

Happy workforce = backbone of Business

Way no. 29 to successful selling

Self-discipline

Self-discipline is another important thing that counts in your sales process.

Lack of discipline will lead to more failures, and result in losing business. Your undisciplined behavior will portray disrespect for others time and your product / service.

A sales professional will surely risk their future if they are not disciplined enough.

Self discipline—A must

Way no. 30 to successful selling

Follow FIFO method for products

FIFO means, First In First Out.

Sell your inventory in the order you receive.

Do not just stack up products and sell any batch from it as per your will. Follow FIFO method for your products, this reduces wastage due to expiry dates.

Keep a proper and easy to understand log of your inventory with proper batch number or serial numbers with its date of manufacturing.

This enhances you to be organized and minimize your losses.

FIFO

Way no. 31 to successful selling

People notice how they are treated

Keep in mind that you are dealing in a social world, and you are constantly being noticed by the way you treat others.

Do not expect others to treat you well for your bad conduct.

Treat others as you expect to be treated.

Example:

If you are expecting a smile from someone, then you need to smile first.

Be fair

Way no. 32 to successful selling

Create a desire of ownership in customers mind

Create a **need** in their mind first and tactfully convert this **need** into **want**.

Make them feel how would their life change after owning your particular product/service?
How happy they will be?
How much time and money they will save?

Paint a picture of your product / service around their virtual world for their visualization purpose. Let them realize how they will be benefited with your product/ service. Let them feel the product.

Examples:

- If you are selling neckless. Just ask your customer to wear it and look in the mirror.
- If you are selling car. Let the customer test drive.

Create desire

Way no. 33 to successful selling

Do not give excuses

Giving excuses is the least thing expected from any sales person. Rather reasoning for a genuine concern is understood, but ensure it does not become a habit, or else you start losing ground.

Instead, be honest and compensate the same.

Example:

Compensate your customer by not charging for a particular dish / drink as you failed to serve their food order on time.

No excuses

Way no. 34 to successful selling

Never ever bad mouth your competitor

Never bad mouth your competitor or his product/service. This is very much un-ethical from business point of view.

Tell superiorities and benefits of your product / service without mentioning any competitor's name or brand. By doing so you are making your product exclusive and non-comparable with others.

Even if customer compares your product/service with competitors, educate him about quality and benefits he will enjoy from your product/service.

Tell people what you got different than others.

All are good but . . .

Way no. 35 to successful selling

Eco friendly things

A very important aspect and prudent practice is to consider Eco friendliness in everything you do. Your presentation material, product / services, packaging, etc. needs to be eco friendly for a very simple reason "save the environment".

Besides, it also adds USP to your sales. Your eco friendliness shows that you respect Mother Nature and share your part of humanity.

Eco friendliness brings respect

Way no. 36 to successful selling

Dress up for calls just as meetings

It is very much necessary, when you are making calls from home. Will you feel fully enthusiastic when you have not taken shower and are making calls sitting on a recliner? The answer is "NO".

Note that, your speech and mentality differs in such situations. Opposite person can recognize the difference and may judge you as an unprofessional sales person.

You are not going to be seen on calls, but do dress up as if you are going for a meeting. This brings authority in your voice over the phone, and you gain confidence and become active.

Be professionally dressed

Way no. 37 to successful selling

Avoid hangovers of elephant sales

It is understood that it takes a lot of effort to make a elephant sales and sales professionals like to celebrate the achievement amongst their team. Celebrating with your team is a must but you also need to be practical enough to make sure this hangover does not take a toll on your performance, and you start taking future sales lightly.

On the contrary make yourself and your team realize that it is just the beginning of such giant sales and buckle up for some more. Do not threaten your future sales with hangovers of elephant sales.

Avoid hangovers

Way no. 38 to successful selling

Send editorials that benefit customers

Send editorials to your customers which could prove beneficial to them.

It can be in form of email, a book, a newsletter, audio/video presentation.

Doing this activity will give you additional appreciation and business from them.

It also adds value to your relationship, and your customer gets the feel of your '**caring attitude**'.

Customer benefits with a better understanding & builds more confidence in the product/services offered.

Keep customers updated

Way no. 39 to successful selling

If you think something is wrong, then something is wrong

Believe in your instinct. If you do not get expected response, do not get sufficient sales, or incomplete sales target, it's time to believe in your instinct, that something is wrong in real.

Just recollect your whole process of sales right from first sales call till customer did not respond, or worse he/she said a big NO.

You need to revamp your entire sales process. Rework at each step involved in sales process and then see the difference of result. Find out your faults and errors, and accordingly apply corrections wherever required.

Instincts

Way no. 40 to successful selling

Sell yourself

Learn to sell yourself to customer.

It all depends on how you present yourself. How you start a conversation with other people which makes them listen to you.

It is your positive approach for which the customer gets sold on.

Always remember, a product/service is valued only because of your presentation skills. You cannot expect a customer to buy Ferrari by an unpleasing personality and inappropriate approach.

Once you are sold, selling your product/service becomes really easy.

Get sold

Way no. 41 to successful selling

All customers are important

All customers are same, as they have shown trust in you and your product/service. So treat all of them similar.

You should not differentiate customers or be racial.
Your sales approach should be ideal and same for everyone.

You need to understand that customers have different requirements depending on their responsibilities and spending habits.

All are equal

Way no. 42 to successful selling

Learn from others mistakes

Do chat with non-performing sales persons occasionally (I have used the word 'occasionally' because if you are in constant touch with them, you too become one).

Try to figure out why he/she failed.

Be smart enough to avoid the same mistakes, which he/she did.

How it helps:

- Serves as warnings
- You know where is the solution
- Differentiates what matter and what does not?
- Recognize your strengths and weaknesses
- Reveals new ideas
- You get the right path and direction
- Shows that we are different from others

2nd mice gets the cheese

Way no. 43 to successful selling

Make it hard for customer to leave you

Provide such a service to your customers that it really becomes difficult for them to go away from you.

For this, you need to sincerely service them, in regards to problem solving, integrity, customer support, consistency, ethics, good attitude, timely delivery, etc.

Value each customers' value.

Hold on to your customers

Way no. 44 to successful selling

You can make things happen

Sales is the only business, where you do not have to wait for things to happen. You can actually make them happen.

Set your own targets, set your own ways of working, set the income you want to earn, and you are good to go.

Since sales is a never ending process, every guidance received, is a new learning. Sales do not have limitations of working hours and the benefits are boundless.

When you get to do things as you want, you have great control on your business and life.

You are the sailor of your ship

Way no. 45 to successful selling

Hire the people you need

We generally tend to hire people we like, whenever we start a new business. But it's the biggest mistake we make. We should hire people we really need in our business, than hiring people we simple like.
Hiring right people is a serious business itself.

Do not ever hire emotionally and understand the reality, it's better to keep a person who understands the business and will add to your business.

Moreover, it is easy to question such people whenever concerned.

Hire skilled staff

Way no. 46 to successful selling

Interview current clients

Interviewing your current customers will give you valuable information which can prove vital for your future sales.

Ask them why they chosen your product/service against competitors?

What according to them is the best element of your product/service?

Do they have any story to share in respect to the product/service? If yes, then you can narrate the same to your future customers during sales.

Ask for testimonials from them. These are of great help.

Interview

Way no. 47 to successful selling

Sell only one thing at a time

If you are having a number of products in your basket, then try to sell only one particular product to a customer. Do not just open up your bag and start displaying everything you have got.

The more products you show, the more will your customer get confused.

The person, who tries to do everything, ultimately achieves nothing.

But if you are selling insurance in morning and running a small eatery in evening, it is exception. It's really acceptable, as you are not mixing both businesses.

One at a time

Way no. 48 to successful selling

People may treat you rudely

At times some people may treat sales people rudely. They may shout at you / bang the door on your face / yell at you not to come/ call again. Even people who know you well, may try to avoid you.

It happens as it is a part of your business. You are in rejection business, do not demoralize yourself. You may tend to lose your temper and wish to respond angrily but this will definitely terminate your chances of approaching them again.

They are not intending to insult you, but just asking you to keep away from them.

It is a rude way of saying "NO THANKS", which some people follow.

Take it easy

Way no. 49 to successful selling

Take Token payment

Token amount is a kind of confirmation from the customer for assurance of buying. You need to practice to ask for token payment whenever a sale is made, to avoid the chances of losing the sale. It also acts as a binding for customer.

You should always consider receiving taken amount in the form of cash or DD. Accepting cheques is an out dated policy

It is an added guarantee of buying to your customers' verbal commitment.

Cement the deal

Way no. 50 to successful selling

Do not interrupt

It's really a bad practice to interrupt someone while he/ she is saying something.

It gives dominating feel to opposite person. It shows that you are not interested in what he/she is saying and forcing them to hear what you want to say.

Interrupting is not going to give business and may result in conflicts.

Allow them to complete their views, then share yours. They are not going to disappear after they are done.

Unless and until you hear them, how are you going to help them solve their issues, understand their needs, provide solutions?

Avoid interruptions

Way no. 51 to successful selling

Look for repeat-business

If you are selling products/services which has limited usability period, or FMCG (Fast Moving Consumer Goods) products, or needs renewals, do look for repeated business from existing customers.

Remember its always easy to sell to a person who is your existing customer, than finding new customers.

Examples:

- Dairy products
- Insurance
- Membership
- Investments
- Garments
- Hospitality

Repeat business with existing customers

Way no. 52 to successful selling

Your time is the most valuable commodity you have

Time is the most valuable commodity you have. So use it properly and wisely, once it's gone, it's gone forever.

Utilize and invest your time appropriately.

Every minute think about growth, and how you can utilize the available free time in a productive manner.

Activities that can be done in free time:
- Reading feedbacks and anticipating
- Organizing files
- Emails
- Updating yourself on business related articles
- Networking through social websites

Remember, *time and tide wait for no men.*

Respect time, and time will respect you

Way no. 53 to successful selling

When in doubt, hold back your actions

Never take any decision/action whenever you are in doubt or uncomfortable about the situation.

Just hold back your actions, and give yourself a cool off period. Then rethink on it and remove all your doubts wisely. If needed take help from your colleagues, boss or close friends.

If, still in doubt; just leave the thing aside. Sometimes it's better to leave things as they are.

Holdback, reassess, take decision

Way no. 54 to successful selling

Recognize new trends of your industry

Whether you are selling your own product/service or some companies', it's necessary to recognize new trends of the product/service. You need to keep pace with the latest trends, otherwise you will be left behind.

Keep sniffing small changes, which have potential to become big later. You need to be in a practice of adapting changes as per time, or later you will fail to do so.

One needs to accept new trends basically for two reasons:

- To sustain in market
- To cope up with customers requirements

Keep pace with the trend

Way no. 55 to successful selling

Do not ever think that you have no competitors

There are competitors for everything.

It will be foolish to think you do not have any competitors, even if you have a fresh product/service.

Even if you are the pioneer of the product/service then also there are hidden competitors. If not now, they will appear much faster than you can think.

People love to copy all successful product/service, as it saves their time and money on research.

No shortage of copy cats

Way no. 56 to successful selling

Ask for the Order

Most of the sales persons do not ask for order after completing the meeting or presentation.

We assume that people have understood everything we have said and we wait for the customer to place the order.

By not asking for order, you are leaving potential customers. Either they will buy from your competitor, or divert their budget into some other product/service, leaving you aside.

So, always ASK for ORDER. There is nothing wrong in asking. You ask and you get. You do not ask and you do not get.

Always ask

Way no. 57 to successful selling

Hunt for bulk orders

Bulk orders always contribute to majority in profits. You save cost of production, transport expenses, convenience in payment, etc. If given proper and satisfactory service, these customers give you constant business.

You can get bulk orders from:

- Communities
- Corporate
- Advertisements
- Special offers
- Family occasions
- Events
- Government bodies

Go for volume

Way no. 58 to successful selling

Make customers feel great

In order to get more from people, help them feel good about themselves.

Everyone likes to be praised for their achievements and personality, and if you contribute in doing so, you are raising their spirits.

Everyone remembers people who made them feel good. Making them feel special creates a comfort zone for positive and healthy discussions.

All this makes customer's feel valued, and in return they help you in accomplishing your goals, i.e., sales.

Appreciate achievements

Way no. 59 to successful selling

Advertising your product properly

Advertising means making people aware about your presence in market.

Choosing the proper media (TV, news papers, magazines, hoardings, leaflets, etc) and territory is a must, otherwise you may not get the desired response.

It helps in brand building and increases sales and the best part is you get end-users or needy customers directly.

Advertising

Way no. 60 to successful selling

Meet decision makers

Before going on any sales meeting make sure you are meeting the right person.

You should be meeting and giving demo/sales pitch only to the people who have decision making powers.

Otherwise you will end up wasting your as well as other people's time, and you may be asked to repeat the whole process again to someone who takes the actual decision for the family/firm.

It not only saves time but it also helps to come to the conclusion more flawlessly.

Be blunt to ask "who takes the decision?"

Decision makers = right people

Way no. 61 to successful selling

Keep your desk / office clean

Create a good and better work place around you.

Keep the work station clean and tidy. Do file all the papers every day before closing the day.

Keep your work area well lit, and ventilated.

Put on some instrumental soothing music on very low volume to create liveliness, and do keep some fragrances flowing. Keep some flowers on table, reception, board room, etc. flowers emit a natural freshness and fragrance.

Be tidy

Way no. 62 to successful selling

Handling Mistakes

We all do commit mistakes, but it is important to handle them in a proper and healthy way.

Studies have shown 95% of what we think never happen, and still we waste our time thinking on it, and get worried.

Go to the root cause of mistake, why it happened, and try to solve it. Study the fact. Many times the cause of mistake is smaller than it appears.

There is nothing wrong in making mistake, but learning from the mistake, and not repeating the same, is what really matters.

Learn from mistakes

Way no. 63 to successful selling

Use emails but don't lose personal touch

It's wise to send details, updates, etc on email to save time and money. But you should not leave the personal touch.

If you can't meet the person, at least make sure you call him and have a chat.

Use latest technologies as added benefit for your business. But do not let it take over and replace you.

Use technology as added benefit

Way no. 64 to successful selling

Make meetings interactive

Always ask questions to bring out what is there in customers mind.

But make sure your questions are relevant to your sales and objections raised by customer.

Your questions should not sound as interrogation. No one likes to be interrogated. So be humble and polite while asking.

Design your questionnaire in such a way that it brings you emotionally closer to the customer.
Implement the agenda with interactive skill. Ensure involvement of all attendees. Your presentation should be designed in such a way that everyone contributes and are kept active.

Whenever you notice cross-talks among participants, politely ask their concerns, to avoid disturbance.

Make customer speak

Way no. 65 to successful selling

Multi-tasking

Though multi tasking is practiced by many professionals in today's date, it is strictly advisable to contemplate following points:

- Only experienced professional should do it
- Primary task should not be affected
- Additional tasks should always be of less weight age
- Avoid confusion
- Try not to take more tasks at a time
- Ensure you are alone while multitasking

AVOID MULTITASKING WHEN IN HAZARDOUS SITUATIONS, like construction sites, factories, driving, laboratory or any other similar situations.

Do only if necessary

Way no. 66 to successful selling

Keep trying

Never give up on any client because they are taking too much of time to close the sale, because time is going to pass anyway, so why not keep trying.

Most of the time the reasons which you get from the customer for not buying are not permanent. Circumstances of customer do change after some time. So never give up on your customer and you will succeed someday.

Very few customers buy on a very first approach. Their "No" should be assumed as "Not Now". A "NO" should not be taken as a setback. Every customer takes time to build confidence in you and your product.

Be inspired and motivated enough to show your never-give-up attitude.

No = Not Now

Way no. 67 to successful selling

Do not count notional profits

A notional profit mainly refers to estimates or speculations gains. Individuals should not ever consider such notional profits as of date's income as they always have chances of failing for some xyz reasons.

Example:

You speculate that your expected earnings for the next month will be xyz amount on sale of 1000 shares. This speculation or estimation may turn incorrect because there may be a twist in market condition. Hence only consider actual profits.

Count actual profit

Way no. 68 to successful selling

Change for positive growth

If changing some strategies or some of your actions brings a fruitful growth, then do not resist.

Positive changes should be always welcomed. Because it's the source of potential growth for your business and prosperity.

Positive changes should be applied as per following situations:

- Fashions and trends
- Economic changes
- Spending habits
- As per region
- As per customer base
- Innovative marketing methods
- Technology

Welcome change

Way no. 69 to successful selling

Cultivate a pleasant tone

Always have a pleasant tone either when talking over the phone or meeting someone in person.

Nobody welcomes a harsh tone and is always taken in offending manner.

Your tone matters a lot in sales as it portrays your emotions for your customer. One cannot say good things in a harsh manner.

Pleasant voice

Way no. 70 to successful selling

Requisites for a star sales performer

Good sales professionals are the ones who quickly learn to present the benefits of product/services to their clients with their dynamic skills, allowing in formation of large networks, quick contacts, and identifying huge number of prospects. They are self starters; believe in team work and master sales in reasonable time.

What makes you a top star sales performer:

- Setting targets/goals
- Setting objectives
- Planning
- Asking valued questions
- Excellent listening and probing
- Best objection handling ability
- Focus and patience
- Leadership
- Solution provider
- Maintaining relationships and after sales services.

Think sales day and night

Way no. 71 to successful selling

Whats IN

The following aspects are IN, in today's sales world:

- Virtual showrooms
- Blogging
- DVD, Online presentation
- Multiple brands
- Media research
- Trials / buy-backs
- 24x7 online stores
- Many comparable products/services
- Free home deliveries
- Order on calls

Trends

Way no. 72 to successful selling

Whats OUT

The following aspects are OUT, from today's sales world:

- Showrooms
- Talking
- Brochures
- Loyalty to single brand
- Recommendations
- Using compulsion
- Limited hours shopping
- Limited variety for comparison
- Personal involvement for delivery
- Queues

Trends

Way no. 73 to successful selling

Keep learning new strategies

You should constantly maintain a learning attitude that helps you adopt new strategies required in your sales business.

Be approachable enough so that everyone can talk to you on a friendly note. This way you will cultivate a habit of learning and make your brain bank filled with new strategies which you can implement during calls / meetings.

Use everything around you and learn to sharpen your skills for implementing the same in your career.

Learn and earn

Way no. 74 to successful selling

Use customers' name
in discussions

Make it a practice to use customers name for at least 3-4 times in first 5-10 minutes of opening the discussion.

It's a known fact; we all feel respected and love to hear our name from other people. Customer gets alert and pays better attention when we use their name often in discussions.

It also gives a feeling to them that you already know them and are talking as a friend and not as an unknown person.

Name sounds beautiful

Way no. 75 to successful selling

Do not drop in without an appointment

This is the worst your customer can expect and should not be done under any circumstances. You strictly have to understand and respect others privacy and ensure you do not close doors permanently for yourself.

Even if you are in same premises and the neighboring person is your close friend, avoid barging in his personal or professional space without prior notice or appointment.

You will definitely risk your relation and ruin the bonding permanently.

Take permission

Way no. 76 to successful selling

Sell benefits

Educate your customers the benefits of features offered in your product/service. When you talk about features its more related to your product/service. But explaining benefits means you are connecting customer with your product/service, as customers are more interested in benefits than features.

As the feature of this book is—its written in simple english and one can start reading it from any page. It is understandable by everyone, even if the person is new in selling business.

Features are general, and benefits may vary from person to person.

Example: a printer with same features can be bought by different customers for different benefits. One may buy for its speed, other may buy for its low power consumption, and someone may buy for its compactness.

Customers buy benefits

Way no. 77 to successful selling

Demo means educating customer

You have to be proactive in explaining the process of using your product / services once your customer has bought them. It's just not showing a slide show or reading out the broucher but a proper training of the entire process.

Educate your customer with complete information like it's uses, do's and don'ts etc. This will cater to your careful attitude and give repeated sales.

Play it

Way no. 78 to successful selling

There are no shortcuts

There are no shortcuts in selling, and do not even try to find any.

Selling is a process, and sometimes it is time consuming, but if you follow certain principles, sale is for sure.

Process may basically include:
- Studying your product
- Short listing buyers
- Making calls
- Fixing appointments
- Handling objections
- Follow ups
- Order closing
- Delivering
- After sales service
- Building rapport
- Asking for referrals

Do not try shortcuts

Way no. 79 to successful selling

Be one step ahead of customer

Be one step ahead of customers' mindset.
Learn to judge customers' reactions and what will be their next move.

Know how to interpret and prepare answers in advance. Instead of customer asking you a question, you give them solutions in advance. Anticipate what they are going to expect from you.

Learn the expertise to read your customers mind and see for yourself the difference in your approaching methods.

Smartness sells

Way no. 80 to successful selling

Invest in quality business cards

Your business card is the identity of your business as well as yours. It gives you and your business an opening.

A good quality and attractive business card has a great impact on people you meet. It should not be fancy. Use good material, colour combinations, design, fonts, etc. It should look unique.

Design it in such a way, that whether people do business with you or not, but they should preserve it. Obviously, when they preserve it, they will considere you someday.

Whenever you present it to someone, they should gaze at it approximately for 15 seconds.

Smart promotional tool

Way no. 81 to successful selling

Easy sales / hard sales

Whenever you come across an easy sale, just analyze what made this sale so easy. Then, create the same conditions for the next sale.

Same goes with hard sale. Whenever you have a hard and difficult sale, analyze the conditions which made this sale so hard and difficult and next time be wise not to create those conditions, or find some easy solution to make such sales easier.

Repeat them

Way no. 82 to successful selling

Your excitement and enthusiasm = your sales

A thumb rule for all the sales. Your excitement is directly proportional to the number of sales you make.

Pass on your enthusiasm to the opposite person.

Low esteem will never bring you good sales figures.

Raise your excitement level to such a height that people around you also get excited.

Professionals have been following this practice to boost their teams' spirit in every field as it motivates everyone around. Many organizations do conduct various sessions/courses for their employees to maintain a higher level of enthusiasm & excitement within.

Be exited and enthusiastic

Way no. 83 to successful selling

You are in REJECTION business

Selling is a rejection business.

You will come across more rejections as compared to acceptance.

One gets rejected nearly 5-6 times before being accepted. It can be 5-6 individual non buyers or 5-6 rejections by the same individual, who takes time to take decision or researches a lot before buying.

It's a fact . . . . accept it . . . . and move ahead . . . .

Do not let rejections shake your confidence.

Take rejections positively

Way no. 84 to successful selling

Make relationship, not sale

By selling your product to a customer you are just making another sale for your living. But by making relationship with them you are making a lifelong partner. Maintaining lifelong relations means more trust, more confidence, more future business and more referrals.

Remember only a few good relations can help you in giving your new product/business a good lift.

Advantages of relationship sales:

- Consistent customer satisfaction
- Brand loyalty
- Word of mouth publicity
- Reliable feedbacks
- Customers feel important
- Reputation and credibility
- Good references
- Saves advertising and marketing expenses

Relations are for life time

Way no. 85 to successful selling

Be honest

Be honest and always be true in whatever you say or do. Honest persons are looked upon as self-respected and they achieve everything they want.

Dishonesty will not take you too far. You can make a few sales but your career will be finished once people realize the truth about you.

Do not think about your benefits, think others benefit first.

Honesty is the best policy

Way no. 86 to successful selling

People buy when they are ready to buy

People buy when they are ready to buy, and not when you want to sell. People will not change their decisions for you.

When do people buy:

- Approached by a trusted sales person
- Referred by a friend/relative
- Festivals/seasons
- Discounts/offers
- Launch of new product
- Financial gains
- When neighbours/friends/relatives buy
- Emotional value
- Security/safety
- Passion
- Need and addiction
- Scarcity
- Future gains
- Prestige

Buyers rule

Way no. 87 to successful selling

Emotional sales

We all are controlled by emotions and feelings. These emotions force us to make decision. You have to understand your customers' emotions which will get them connected to the product / service, eventually closing a sale.

Emotional factors that will help you win a sale are:

Beliefs	Faith	Leadership
Belonging	Fear	Love
Care	Gratification	Pride
Competition	Greed	Shame
Desire	Guilt	Trend setting
Enthusiasm	Happiness	Trust
Envy	Hope	Value

Helpful emotions

Way no. 88 to successful selling

Take Responsibility

Take responsibility in everything you do, or say.

Be responsible for your sale and after sales service.

This will build trust and help you get repeated orders or referrals from clients.

Taking responsibility will help you in the following ways:

- Increase your credibility
- Shows your seriousness
- Achieve targets
- Increase efficiency
- Grow sales
- Decision making
- Cater good services
- Customer satisfaction

You are responsible

Way no. 89 to successful selling

Use words ending with ER-EL-EST

Barter	Fuel	Offer
Best	Greatest	Owner
Better	Happiest	Parcel
Biggest	Higher	Power
Broader	Honest	Propel
Channel	Interest	Quicker
Compel	Invest	Request
Excel	Largest	Sober
Fastest	Latest	Stronger
Feel	Leader	Test
Finest	Lowest	Winner

Significant words

Way no. 90 to successful selling

There is always a next time

Do not expect all the deals will be closed in first meeting. People tend to buy time to take decisions.

You may be called next time for closing or maybe you need to carry some additional information in next meeting. So, be prepared to have multiple meetings or calls for a single deal.

Before concluding the meetings make sure you have got assurance/surety of next meeting with a confirmed date. Let the customer know what you would be expecting in the next meeting and take the conversation to next level. This ensures customers involvement and you are on his mind.

Your next opportunity to see the customer also allows you to go prepared for any un-answered objections/queries raised in your first meeting.

Better luck next time

Way no. 91 to successful selling

Congratulating customers

Whenever you come across the news of your customers' achievement, do drop him a hand written card to congratulate him.

This way customer feels appreciated, and surely it will strengthen your relations.

Congratulations

Be a well wisher

Way no. 92 to successful selling

Remember names

Remember names of people you meet. So, whenever you see them next time, you greet them by their name.

People appreciate that you remember names, and this gives them a personal feeling of respect and honor.

But make sure you pronounce name properly, or else, it becomes a bad show.

Nothing is more delighting than hearing your correct name from other person.

Use proper salutations with respect to the individual. Examples—Dr., Captain, Major, Professor, etc. Neglecting such salutations makes the other person feel offended.

Proper addressing

Way no. 93 to successful selling

Meet at customers' convenience

It's better to see customer at his office or home. Do not expect people to come to your place to listen to your sales oration and buy your product/service.

Be flexible with your meetings. People do not like to waste their time, and prefer door step service.
Let the customer decide the time and venue of meeting, do not force yours on them.

If you are really occupied, tell them politely and request to reschedule.

Customers are always glad when you understand their situations and adjust accordingly.

Go to customer

Way no. 94 to successful selling

Associate with good people

Get into habit of being with right people. Always associate yourself with good/reputed/successful people. It increases your trustworthiness and such people surely contribute to your success.

You are known by what company you keep. People judge your credentials by this. Associate with people who have positive attitude, dreams to grow big, ready to share and help. Being with such people will encourage you to adopt their way of dealing with challenges. This will definitely benefit your personality in a positive and respectable manner.

If you do not have good people in your social/friend circle, you better be alone, rather than being in bad company.

Right people = your success

Way no. 95 to successful selling

Watch audio/video of successful businessmen

Ever noticed, while watching romantic scenes you too become romantic. Same way violent scenes make your mind violent.

Your mind behaves/reacts to what it listens/sees.

So, listening or watching videos of successful and great personalities, you can train your mind to think success.

If your mind wants you to become successful, you will ultimately become one.

Watching/listening has a great effect on human behavior.

Be inspired

Way no. 96 to successful selling

Essentials of a feedback form

A typical feedback form should include the following points:

1. Customer details
2. Was accurate information provided?
3. Was quality of product/service satisfactory?
4. Why chosen your product/service than competitors?
5. Were terms & conditions / warrantee / maintenance explained properly?
6. Did our product serve the purpose?
7. Was delivery on time?
8. Areas of improvement
9. Overall experience in star ratings.
10. Will you recommend this product/service to your friends/relatives?
11. If "YES" for point no. 10, then 2 referrals.
12. If "NO" for point no. 10, then reason.

Take feedback

Way no. 97 to successful selling

What more can you do?

Always ask yourself these questions without fail before closing the day.

- What could you do better to get better results?
- What you did today, was it enough? Or you could have added more to it to get more numbers?
- How could you improve yourself?
- Do you need to change the way of approach?
- What will be the effects of applying xyz strategy to increase sales?
- Do you want to make any changes in product / services?

Fruitful day

Way no. 98 to successful selling

Do not repeat call instantly

If a person is not picking your call for the first time, or has disconnected it, please do not call him instantly. Give a good 15-30 minutes break in between 2 calls. The person may be occupied with some important work, and if they do not answer unknown numbers, please ensure to drop a text message, mentioning your name and purpose of calling, in not more than 3-4 lines.

It's very unprofessional to call anyone for more than 2 times in a day, if the opposite person has not answered your calls.

Whenever they pick up your call start with sentences like—I hope this is the right time to talk / hope I am not disturbing you.

Telephone etiquettes

Way no. 99 to successful selling

Write down point's immidietly after call / meeting

We tend to forget 20-30% of what we discussed with customer on phone or in meeting and many times this forgotten 20-30% includes some important points.

Habit of writing down, immediately after you keep the receiver, or come out of customers' office, will make sure that you do not miss out on anything.

As the discussion is fresh in mind, it's easier to recollect all the information instantly.

Pen it down

Way no. 100 to successful selling

So what if people call u a day dreamer?

Always dream big . . . . you can't achieve what you want without dreaming.

Day dreaming is a creative act, which helps you visualize your plans and goals.

All you need to follow, are these 3 key essentials:

- Thought process
- Writing points
- Implementing

Daydreaming helps you in brainstorming of new ideas. Taking small breaks of daydreaming before any major decisions, stimulates your mind to wander into infinite number of possibilities without any limitations.

Daydreaming is necessary

Way no. 101 to successful selling

If you fail to plan, then you are planning to fail

It is a must to plan in everything you do. Your success and achievements are all designed on the basis of a well planned programme. If there is no proper planning done, you are very much susceptible to come across difficulties or barriers that will hinder your end result.

It is very rightly said that if you fail to plan, than you are planning to fail because unknowingly you are diverted to the path that directs you down because you have not planned about how to curb up from situations, you are not able to take control over unplanned circumstances ultimately resulting in failure.

Planning a must

Way no. 102 to successful selling

Wear a smile

Always smile, while introducing yourself, as well as while explaining your product/service.

Remember, it's your fist step to get in any relation.

Studies have proved that people remember a smiling face in the long run, than a rude and angry face.

It brings comfort to open up the discussion from customers' side.

And the best thing about smile is that you can use it as many times as you want, without any investment, and it is the easiest way to narrow down differences, if any.

People love and remember smiling faces

Way no. 103 to successful selling

Doubt the person who buys without any objection & negotiation

In today's world of competition, every individual wants to achieve the No. 1 ranking, and many do end up following cunning practices like copying.

You need to be smart enough in analyzing people who pretend to be customers and end up buying your products / services without any hesitation. They may have intentions to gather your information and study on the product / service to be implemented by them.

Be alert

Way no. 104 to successful selling

Read books of selling/ marketing guru's

You really do not need to waste time in experimenting. Many successful people in this world have shared their techniques and experiences, etc in books/blogs. Reading their books/blogs will definitely help you in acquiring some of the best techniques for selling of your products / services.

Invest your time in reading atleast for 30 minutes daily.

Advantages of reading are:

- Knowledge
- Improves creativity
- Sharpens skills
- Good vocabulary

All leaders are readers

Way no. 105 to successful selling

Take a long term view

Look for maintaining long term relations with people you meet and existing customers too.

Do not take sales as a onetime activity. It's going to work for years. Once you get into the trust circle of people, just maintain it, and you will get business and repeated business from these people.

Most of the time, people who trust you, do not even bother to search for other sales people for their service. They will just depend on you for your product/service.

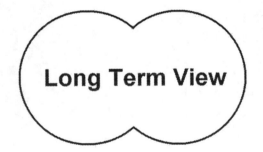

Long term relations

Way no. 106 to successful selling

Nobody will believe, until you believe

Believing in yourself is a great motivator. When you believe in yourself, you gain confidence and ability to convince customers.

You start visualizing success, overcome barriers and ensure that you contribute value added ideas for your customer.

Believing in yourself will help you in several ways, like:

- Never give up attitude (improves consistency)
- Accepting challenges
- Positive nature
- Customers belief and trust
- You are the leader
- Adds to goodwill
- Increase in sales

Your belief is your strength

Way no. 107 to successful selling

Confirm appointment before going

It is a good practice to take a confirmation again for the same appointment because of several reasons:

- Other person may have forgotten due to his busy schedule
- You might unknowingly take an appointment on a holiday.
- Your customer might get an emergency
- Customer might want to reschedule after an hour due to a delay in existing meet.
- A customer may ask you to bring some additional info, which was needed in meeting.

Take confirmation

Way no. 108 to successful selling

These actions disturb

Some of the actions/behaviors which distract / disturb an ongoing conversation / meeting:

- Ringing cell phones, text message beep
- Presence of a non participant
- Scratching neck, elbow, head etc
- Eyelid drooping
- Informal talks with colleague
- Distributing presentation materials in meeting
- Eatables / drinks
- Power failures
- Adjusting room lights / air conditioners etc.
- Participants' lack of attention
- Lengthy unwanted discussions
- Improper agenda
- Late comers
- Informal gestures and casual attitude of any participant.

It disturbs

Way no. 109 to successful selling

It's not what you have; it's what people think you have

You need to understand that everything you represent is creating your image on others. You are made up of your acts and beliefs that make the other person characterize you.

Example:

A person from hotel industry randomly taking personal care of his visitors, will always be considered because customers have framed an image that shows his hospitality in serving quality food, mouthwatering taste, value for money, overwhelming attitude for customer satisfaction.

Win hearts

Way no. 110 to successful selling

To improve, learn to acknowledge your mistakes

No one is perfect in this world and mistakes do happen, but acknowledging mistakes and learning from them is an opportunity to prove yourself.

Accepting mistakes has the following advantages:

- Avoids problems from turning into big ones
- Learning
- People respect you for accepting your mistake
- Teaches you to take responsibility
- You do not tend to repeat same mistakes
- Makes you strong
- Boosts self respect
- Shows your ethical values
- Helps you strive for perfection

Accepting mistakes is not going to put you down in anyway.

Accepting mistake = not being stupid

Way no. 111 to successful selling

Add your personal guarantee

Extend actual guarantee of your product / services with your personal guarantee. It adds value to your product / service. Customers feels more satisfied and values your personal touch.

When you show confidence in your product / service, your customer gets sold for the same, as he feels that you have experienced it. It portrays as a personal guarantee from your end on your product /service.

Personal guarantee

Way no. 112 to successful selling

Rehearse for presentations

Rehearsal for any presentation plays a vital role in any sales. Customers have full attentions on what you are saying as well as your gestures.

Points to remember while rehearsing:

- Memorize your opening and closing sentences.
- Write down whatever you wish to speak.
- Record yourself while rehearsing
- Ask your team mates to observe and give feedback.
- Review your presentation material
- Rehearse atleast 4-5 times.
- Rehearse in front of a mirror.
- Keep in mind the length of your presentation
- Dress rehearse at least once.
- Keep in mind the number of people attending your presentation.
- Include some humour while presentation
- Be relaxed

Rehearse

Way no. 113 to successful selling

Do not start with the price first

Discussing about price in the beginning of a call/meeting means negative results. You are definitely making your customer feel uncomfortable if you start with the price factor. Your customer will feel offended and this will surely spoil your credit in market.

Pricing should be mentioned at the end of the complete presentation and it should be effectively applied that your customer remains strongly connected to your product / service rather than its price.

Price not first

Way no. 114 to successful selling

Bad experiences are necessary for your growth

Keep learning from your bad experiences.

Many a times we just get tensed by bad experiences but never try to figure out why it really happened.

Once you know the reason of failure, you will be able to take a wise decision next time.

The experiences which we consider bad, are really necessary for certain growth. Worth of such experiences is realized after passing that bad patch, and not immediately.

Most of the successful businessmen have overcome from many bad experiences before becoming successful.

"Suffering is necessary until it is unnecessary."
—Eckhart Tolle

Success never comes easy

Way no. 115 to successful selling

High clicked websites

Take advantage of social websites such as linked' in, Facebook, Twitter . . . etc. you will see yourself in limelight. Your daily posts and advertisements will surely help you in generating curiosity amongst the users, as these websites are highly clicked.

Managing your page on such websites is very similar to displaying your product / service in any exhibition or for the targeted audience. Writing blogs and statements will involve public attention and triumph in making huge sales.

Click . . . Click . . . Click . . .

Way no. 116 to successful selling

I CAN . . . . these 2 words are very important

These 2 powerful words will generate enthusiasm, positive energy, ideas & skills to think on how you are going to offer your product/services to clients and close the deals.

These 2 words will give you **Will** of doing anything.

Your desire to sell should be more than the fear of getting rejected.

When you nourish your brain with I CAN, it finds ways that IT CAN. On the other hand, what happens when you think of I CAN'T, your brain starts finding ways that IT CANT, and it will continuously give you these ways until it's really a I CANT.

Just say "I CAN"

Way no. 117 to successful selling

Do not drink, smoke or gamble

Its known facts that people staying away and alone or with same gender groups, get addicted to drinking, smoking or gambling. Their loneliness in non-working hours and friend circle pushes them into such activities.

Instead, whenever you are away from your home for business, keep yourself occupied in evenings, in some other activities such as watching movie, going for a stroll, visiting new places around, etc. Such activities will keep you busy and away from unwanted addictions.

Be busy

Way no. 118 to successful selling

Feel good factor is essential

It adds charm on your face while presenting yourself to the customer.

Feel good factor should be exercised seriously as it adds to boost your self-confidence and beliefs. Every sales professional has to rigorously practice it as they have to meet many people for their business.

Feel good factor helps you enhance your capacities in following manner:

- It builds up your motivation
- Maintains good health
- Ensures optimum productivity
- Visible self improvement
- Huge appreciation

Feel Good

Way no. 119 to successful selling

Selling is getting connected with people

Selling is regarded as the best way to get connected with people. It creates opportunities to explore yourself and get introduce to new markets.

You should always consider yourself to be lucky for being in 'sales industry' as it is the only industry to help you venture infinite possibilities.

Selling offers an individual the most blessed gateway to bond with people.

Get connected

Way no. 120 to successful selling

When to let go a prospective

Sometimes it may become obvious to let go a prospective customer for the following reasons:

- The person did not answer your calls, even after repeated trying.
- The person just wanted to gather knowledge of your product.
- Your competitors have approached with some better deal than yours.
- Customers have some personal and genuine reasons for not buying.
- When customer expects unrealistic bargains and negotiations.
- When customer gives lame excuses and reasons for not buying.
- When you realize his fake identity.

Non prospective = waste of time

Way no. 121 to successful selling

Your sales funnel should always be full

Your sales funnel should be always full with good number of leads, prospects and customers. Have more people on your meeting/calling list so that you never fall short of business.

Always keep adding new contacts through referrals, advertisements, seminars, etc.

Maximum contacts = maximum Business

Way no. 122 to successful selling

Be ambitious

Being ambitious and determined to sale are crucial initial steps in sales process.

If you have a strong desire to achieve you targets and goals, you simply need to be ambitious to make all your dreams come true . . .

Your eagerness or high desire to achieve something makes your ambition grow powerful.

You can boost your ambition by implementing:

Self esteem and confidence
Thinking about your inner values and goals
Practical behavior and your social impact
With best knowhow of competition
Strictness in work
Improvements

Ambitions, a necessity

Way no. 123 to successful selling

Make as many as good friends as you can

Friends help in each other's business growth and friendship is an indirect sales process.

Take good care of your friends, and they will take care of your sales, either by buying or recommending you to their relatives / friends.

Making friends refers to bonding of trust in new relationships. Once this trust is made you surely make way to achieve multiple sales.

Friendship rewards

Way no. 124 to successful selling

Leave your bad attitude

Attitude is the biggest wall between 'Yes and No' for a deal. Amongst 3 essentials of business (attitude, confidence and faith) attitude is the most vital element affecting sales.

No one in this world like individuals with a bad attitude.

Even employees of any company do not like their boss with a bad attitude.

If you want to keep any attitude, then keep a good attitude, it brings good sales. Positive attitude always boosts your performance and releases positive vibes around.

Attitude matters

Way no. 125 to successful selling

Do not allow people to waste your time

Many times you are on your way to meet prospective client, and you happen to meet your friend, colleague or even relative, be smart to spend only 1-2 minutes in exchanging greetings only.

They may not be aware of your schedule, and tend to keep talking a bit more than usual. It's your job to excuse yourself as early as possible to avoid your business loss.

Because a delay of 15 minutes also causes a chain of adjournment's for the whole day.

Your time is important

Way no. 126 to successful selling

Always carry a note pad and Pen / pencil with you

Get into habit of carrying a small note pad and pen/ pencil wherever you go, even if you are going out with family/friends/non-official work etc.

You never know, where you may get a new idea, opportunity, or some contact numbers on hoardings/ newspapers, etc, which may be useful for you in future.

Following this practice will help you in avoiding inconvenience of searching the information when needed.

Due to advancement in technology you can even use mobiles/note pads for this purpose, as per your choice and comfort.

Make notes

Way no. 127 to successful selling

People do not want cheap product

People do not buy cheap products / services, but need good stuff at fair price. Do not sell / promote cheap product / service.

Only cheap products / services would have been in existence in market, if customers had such choices.

The truth is customers majorly consider the products / services quality, brand, durability, urgency etc while buying.

Reliable products

Way no. 128 to successful selling

Customers rate TRUST as no.1 requirement

The key for every successful sale is TRUST.
Customers will not buy from you if they do not trust you, or have lost trust in you. When you keep up to your commitments and consistently deliver the best, TRUST is developed naturally.

The following requisite is the recipe to build TRUST:

- Resonate
- Good illustration/demonstration/presentation
- Punctuality
- Past experiences
- Goodwill in market
- Superior and reliable product / service
- Excellent after sales service
- Transparence
- "You Care" attitude

All businesses run on trust

Way no. 129 to successful selling

Do not discuss your business plans with everyone

Sales professionals do tend to share their ways of business to others unknowingly, it is accordingly copied and practiced by others, resulting in ending their potential market.

You have to be smart enough in not sharing your plans or business policies to any outsider because it will definitely affect you adversely.

You have to maintain secrecy in every business as it is your bread and butter that cannot be shared with anyone.

Maintain secrecy

Way no. 130 to successful selling

Closing questions

When you are finished with your presentation and cleared all the objections, it's time to ask for a close now. Many sales persons expect that the customer will revert back if he/she wants to buy, and do not bother to ask for a close.

Few closing questions, which can help you get instant buying signals:

1. What do you think now?
2. How far are you from decision making?
3. Is there anything more?
4. How soon can we go ahead with formalities?
5. I believe our product/service fulfils your expectations.
6. And we have a special offer until dd-mm-yy.

Take confirmation before leaving

Way no. 131 to successful selling

Do not see your product as a commodity

Your product / service is the basis of your sales and you have to create its own worth or the customers will just look at it as a commodity.

The best way is to connect your product / service emotionally to your customer, by proving its benefits for them. You have to give existence to your product / service in such a manner that every customer desires to make them a part of their life.

Remember, It is your skill that adds value and life to a particular product / service and creates a need for all.

Bring life to your product

Way no. 132 to successful selling

Do not be afraid to try new idea

Trying new ideas explores potential opportunities for growing your sales.

You never know which one idea may change your business drastically.

Many times we just want to continue with some tried and tested ideas and are not willing to try something new to increase business due to fear of failure.

We just take for granted that the new idea may not click, or how will others react to your idea?

In such situations, do not ever think about others, think what happens if you see some other person coming with same idea somewhere someday and getting tremendous positive response. Then nothing is left with you other than regretting.

New ideas

Way no. 133 to successful selling

Needy people

The best mathematic in sales is to discover right people for your product / service, Find who are in need and try to be the first one to approach them.

Like at the start of winter season, if you are the first one to start selling room heaters, with some new features than last year, you will get good response.

Targeting right people at right time will help you make sales throughout the tenure.

Search needy buyers

Way no. 134 to successful selling

Focus on your target

You have to be strongly focused on your targets / goals, as your negligence will cause failure. Your focus acts as a supplement to achieve your target. Once you are focused, your targets / goals are locked in memory and makes your sales easily possible. Studies have proven a strongly focused sales professional does not let anything affect their target; they keep getting updated on real time basis, narrowing their path towards the end goal.

If you divert your attention, you lose command on your focus and lead yourself to failure. Your targets / goals will never be accomplished if you get distracted by common calamities that are a part and parcel of every individual's life.

You lose the focus, and you lose the target. You can't hit the target, which you can't see.

Do not lose your focus

Way no. 135 to successful selling

Good relationship = good sales

Instead of building clientele, build a relationship.
When you approach a customer with the intention to make sales, you are very much prone to failure.

Whereas when you try to bond a new relationship with them, it results in your favor in the long run.
Keeping a good relationship with all customers will increase your sales exponentially.

Building relations not only helps you win business from that particular customer but also advantages you with the opportunity to explore their network.

Build relations

Way no. 136 to successful selling

Plan multiple appointments in same territory

It is advisable that you do not fix appointments inappropriately. Appointments for your day should be arranged in such a manner that you make the optimum use of your valuable time.

Planning your appointments in same territory will definitely help you meet maximum customers, with limited efforts avoiding traveling exertion and delay in your visits.

Multiple appointments in same area will maintain your momentum and tempo of high enthusiasm, obtaining best results for the day.

It also adds to branding as it creates the awareness amongst the people about your presence.

Make the best

Way no. 137 to successful selling

Keep a good balance of deals

Your one big deal could contribute to a good percentage of overall income. But small deals are necessary too, to maintain a good balance.

Practically one big deal is a must in 10-15 deals.
And 1 average deal after every 3-4 small deals

Small deals help you maintain the cash flow of your business and always easy to achieve. Understanding to maintain the balance is the key to bring stability in business.

Mix small, average and big deals

Way no. 138 to successful selling

Practice self-praise method before going for meeting

Make a habit of talking to yourself, may be in front of the mirror.

Praise yourself that you are knowledged and experienced and are going to crack this deal, you are very good at it, you have done this before, it's easy for you, etc. All this will help you in building confidence.

There are good chances that you will come across some of your weaknesses, which can be improved while you practice.

This will enable your mind to gather all positive thoughts and energy to give a impressive presentation.

You can do it

Way no. 139 to successful selling

Awareness vs. sales

Awareness of your product in market and sales is interrelated in many ways. But the combination of these two components should be blended perfectly.

Few points to be noted for this:

- Low awareness + Low Growth = bad sales + bad branding
- Low awareness + high growth = good sales + bad branding
- High awareness + low growth = bad sales + good branding
- High awareness + high growth = good sales + good branding

Understand and act accordingly

Way no. 140 to successful selling

Study customer / company profile in advance

Being prepared with all information is very vital before every call or meeting. It's a proven fact that things are positively materialized when you know about the opposite individual/organization.

One needs to be thoroughly prepared with the following checklist well in advance:

- Do they qualify for your product/service?
- Understanding their business.
- Studying their annual reports
- Their likes/dislikes/hobbies
- How your product/service will benefit them
- Their budget
- Their future plans
- Their decision making process
- Current vendor, if any?
- Their rapport in market

They feel you know them, and it helps in bonding

Way no. 141 to successful selling

Work ethically

Be ethical in everything you do. Non-ethical practices will make sales but your rapport and your existence will vanish very soon.

People really do not mind spending a bit extra time and money while buying from a ethical sales person rather than a person who just wants to push sales by hook or crook.

NOTE : Unethical practices will surely lead you to suffer legal consequences.

Sell honestly

Way no. 142 to successful selling

If appropriate, share your home contact number

Sometimes you may feel the need to share your home contact number with a few selective prime customers.

This is not necessary and depends from person to person to act upon. It becomes essential if the client is aggressive and you have limited time to get the sales done. Be selective in sharing your home number as it may be misused for general follow ups by the customer.

Let you family members know the name of your customer who is expected to call.

Note: Be very careful in doing so, as it may intrude your privacy and your family members may not really appreciate this.

Being personal . . . some times

Way no. 143 to successful selling

It should be a conversation

Give sufficient time to customers to talk. The golden rule of listening twice than you speak is of great help.

Listening to customers make them feel that you are giving importance to what they are saying. It shows that you are really connected and concerned for them.

Ever wondered why you have a pair of ears and a mouth?

Let customer speak

Way no. 144 to successful selling

Answer calls within 3-4 rings

It's necessary to answer the phone quickly within 3-4 rings.

Add a smile while picking up the phone, it polishes your tone and it can be sensed by the other person.
Do keep a habit of greeting and make the other person feel welcomed.

Politely ask his/her name and proceed.

If you need to forward your customers' call to some other person in your team, then inform them the team members' name before transferring the call because if the call gets dropped / disconnected while transferring, it will help your customer to get connected again.

Call portrays you

Way no. 145 to successful selling

Do not ever do sympathy sales

Do not talk about your personal problems (relationship/ finances) with customers to get sales done.

Very few people fall for sympathy and do the deals. Even if they do, they will someday regret buying from you.

You will not be able to maintain a healthy and trustworthy relationship with such clients.

Customers will not only ignore you but also pass on a negative message against you.

No sympathy sales

Way no. 146 to successful selling

Always reach 10 to 15 minutes before time

It is extremely important to respect time, yours as well as others. Being punctual leads to several benefits such as :

- Shows you are disciplined
- Builds confidence
- Reveals humility and humbleness
- Shows you care
- Strengthen relations
- Shows professionalism
- Optimum productivity
- Credibility & Reliable
- You get extra time to interact with other people around.
- Your scheduled activities for the day are accomplished.
- Customer is more than happy to share references.

Punctuality pays good rewards

Way no. 147 to successful selling

Always lead the discussion positively

You may come across instances where people in the meeting are discussing negative topic with each other. You need to take initiative to break down the negative conversation and lead the discussion in a positive manner.

Do not bring up unconstructive topics, even if the customer starts something, this may lead to negativity in discussion and ruin the agenda of meeting.

Just learn to divert it cleverly.

Keep discussions positive

Way no. 148 to successful selling

Always carry your business card

We all have come across the situation of not carrying our business card due to negligence or while enjoying holidays, or running out of stock while on long business tour.

You never know when a customer turns up. It's really awkward reprehensible situation when you cannot introduce yourself officially.

Primary purpose of carrying business card is to present yourself, but not to forget, it also acts as a gate pass to prove your identity for entry in homes and offices of customers.

Note: whatever the reason of not carrying your business card, it reflects your carelessness.

Introduce yourself

Way no. 149 to successful selling

Old enquiry list

It is the list of people who responded to your newspaper advertisement, or had attended your exhibition and showed some interest, but didn't buy from you for some reasons.

Your product might not have been their priority at that time, but it might be later.

Though the chances are few that these people will call you. But keeping them updated once in a while about your products/service is worth a try.

Recall everyone

Way no. 150 to successful selling

Do not interrogate, just ask questions to client

In order to gather essential information and offer proper guidance, questioning is required. Questions that you have in mind in order to make a sale should be welcoming and should not be annoying.

One needs to be tactful enough to play words in a manner where it sounds more like a conversation rather interrogation.

Your tone and pitch should be pleasing enough to make your customer comfortable in answering your questions without any hesitation. Harsh tone and high pitched voice while questioning makes the other person feel interrogated.

Many times the customer will not share some personal issues with you. You need to understand such issues and should not repeatedly ask that question. Understand customers' unspoken answers too.

No one likes to be interrogated

Way no. 151 to successful selling

Sponsor events for social cause

Sponsor some events for good social cause.

Like—sponsoring cloth/food etc to old age homes, adoption agencies.

Marathon to raise money for flood donation camps, charities, etc.

It works in mutual benefits. It serves both the ends. Needy ones get help and you get publicity. This in turn will increase your business.

Sponsor events

Way no. 152 to successful selling

Call @ right time

You have to take precautions while calling someone with regards to their timings, as your call may become a disturbance and you might lose your prospective customers' business.

Customers are professionals from variety of fields and have different working hours uncommon to you, hence it is essential to respect their time and proceed with your call (interest).

Examples:

- Doctor's will prefer calls in late evenings
- Lawyer's prefer calls on weekend
- People working in night shifts prefer calls in day time

Call at customers' preference

Way no. 153 to successful selling

Do not give too much time to a single customer

Just keeping on talking without listening or understanding the customers will have adverse effects on your sales in the following ways:

- You may reveal your weakness
- Customer feels insignificant
- You are imposing your ideas on customers
- Customer will never open up
- You get exhausted
- Customer will not value you
- Customer will try to avoid you in future
- You fail to sell

Hold your horses

Way no. 154 to successful selling

Convince people that you have the best

It is easier to convince people that no one has got such product / service what you have, rather than convincing that you have better product/service than others.

Do not compare your product/service with others.

You need to prove the potential of your product/service by stating its benefits.

Keep increasing his wants and eagerness in your product/service by offering him creative solutions.

Showing them testimonial letters from your existing customers will prove beneficial.

No one has got what you have

Way no. 155 to successful selling

Do not be single tracked for big sale

Elephant sales are necessary, but do not waste time chasing a big order. You may miss out many small sales which could cumulatively bring huge profits.

Big sales are difficult, as they involve big people/corporate and a big monitory transaction which make the entire process difficult.

You should take big orders as and when they come while fishing for smaller ones. But do not just run after them.

Small is beautiful

Way no. 156 to successful selling

What triggers window shopping

- Product display
- Sales persons' selling skills
- Packaging
- Pricing
- Physically feeling the product
- Information broucher in the store
- Brand of product
- Offers and schemes
- Seasonal requirements
- Spending habits with regards to certain age.
- Festivals
- Place & location
- Needs
- Influence
- Limited edition
- Fashion
- Leisure and boredom
- Emotional triggers

Window shopping—a boom

Way no. 157 to successful selling

Approach your friends and relatives when new in business

Selling to a completely unknown person is very difficult, especially if you have started new business.

Friends and your own relatives will buy from you quickly than others. Simple reason behind this is that these people TRUST YOU.

They know your genuineness. And this is what makes them buy.

When your friends and relatives are satisfied by your product/service ask them for referrals. And they will be more than happy to give you one.

Trust brings sales

Way no. 158 to successful selling

Do not pre-judge any customers by their appearance

Many times you come across individuals who are contradictory to their appearance. This creates confusion in our mind regarding their buying potentials/ credentials/ behavior etc.

We need to avoid such incorrect pre-judgments & follow our sales principles as we practice with the other potential customers.

Such incorrect pre-judgments always initiates negative approach which leads to a poor sale. We need to focus every individual as a prospect buyer and approach accordingly.

Individuals differ

Way no. 159 to successful selling

Difference between bargaining and negotiation

Bargaining means agreeing on certain price. Here sales person gets only his margin and nothing else. In bargaining the buyer usually benefits more than you. *This cultivates buyer-seller relations.*

Negotiation means giving something in exchange of something. Like, if you give discount, you ask customer to buy more quantity. In negotiation both the parties win. *This cultivates partnership relations.*

Negotiations are always recommendable, as it keep both the parties happy.

Create win-win situation

Way no. 160 to successful selling

Do not give false promises to customers

Only promise what you can deliver. False promises will impact your sales in a big way.

False promises will have following impact on your sales:

- Poor reputation in market
- Loss of trust
- Very small time benefit
- Competitors gain
- Limited future and growth
- Legal complications
- Penalties
- It affects your colleagues/company/product
- Financial loss
- Stress

False promises = loss of business

Way no. 161 to successful selling

The person who asks price first, will not buy

Customers who are serious buyers, generally examine the products / services and then talk about price factor. Their main motto to buy a particular product / service is its benefits, and that attract their attention. After reviewing it they justify its worth with the price tag.

Customers who directly ask for the price or check the price tags are not keen buyers. They actually do not have any intentions of buying, and reason the same with price tags.

It will always be too costly for them.

Window shoppers

Way no. 162 to successful selling

A "NO" should never demoralize you

Be practical, every individual whom you meet or call will not buy your product/service. Why will he?

Do you buy things just because u got a call, or the gentleman approached you? I know u do not. so why others will?

When you hear a "NO", just relax . . .
A "YES" is just around the corner . . .

Next time when you hear a "NO", you think and plan how in the next call or meeting you will work hard to hear a "YES".

A "NO" should make you work harder and harder.

"NO" brings you more closer to a deal

Way no. 163 to successful selling

Copy customers' postures and words

In order to make your customer feel that you are fully in synch with them, you need to learn the tactful skills to copy their posture and words to use them during your conversation.

This should be applied smartly ensuring, it should not seem as you are making fun / mimicking your customer. It will help you to connect strongly and win your customers confidence in buying your product / service.

Bond well

Way no. 164 to successful selling

You never get a 2nd chance for your 1st impression

Your 1st impression is your last impression.

Dress yourself like a star business person, people will take you seriously.

Do present your business card with both the hands, and that too when you are standing.

If you have already taken seat, then lift yourself a bit from chair while exchanging business cards.

Your appearance talks for you.

You are the brand ambassador of your product/services.

Dress for your success.

Be presentable

Way no. 165 to successful selling

Give feedback to referrers

Keeping your referrers informed on the development with their references is very important.
This will help in maintaining good and long lasting relations between you two and they will help you with more new references in future.

Once you share the status of your discussion with the prospective customer to the referrer, it gives them a chance to convince the prospective customer for buying your product / service. This is a small team work that helps you to achieve good business.

Update your activities

Way no. 166 to successful selling

Be an active listener

Listening is the skill to receive & interpret messages correctly in every communication process.

First give time to people to express themselves.
Acknowledge their concerns at regular intervals.
Your conscious effort towards listening ensures improvement in productivity and influence negotiations.

You cannot sale your product/service just by starting your sales presentation instantly. First listen to customers' needs and wants. Your job becomes easy after listening to them.

Avoid distractions while listening, as the customer may feel offended. Your active listening skills, will lead to a healthy and fruitful conversation with customers.

Listen to people

Way no. 167 to successful selling

Do not repeat topic, unless asked

Whenever on call, demo or in meeting, do not repeat a topic unless asked for. It show's your un-preparedness. Customers may think you do not have sufficient marketing stuff and are not fully prepared resulting loss of confidence in your product / services offered.

Repeating words every time irritates customers and may also degrade your presentation. You will definitely miss big possibilities if you stammer or roll same words during your sales approach.

Stop repeating

Way no. 168 to successful selling

Taking feedback is major key point for future sales

Always remember to take feedback from people who buy your product / services. It will help you know what are your and your products good qualities, and why they purchased it.

Call people who did not buy from you. They are important too. They will tell you what they did not like about you or your product / service.

Expect informal feedback also, as many customers hate to fill the feedback form or answer feedback questionnaire.

All this will help you in improving sales in future.

Three Modes of feedbacks:
- In person
- Through email
- IVR

Take feedback

Way no. 169 to successful selling

Do not get tired and give up too soon

At times you may feel exhausted that you have been chasing to achieve your targets or cracking a big deal like a bulk order from Xyz Company. Ensure you do not give up on that particular job as your every effort is simply bringing you more closer to the deal.

You have to rigorously follow the activity until you succeed as it is only going to take some more time and efforts. Your patience to hold on the bar is at test when such situations arise.

You may be too close to the deal

Way no. 170 to successful selling

Identify the right people fit for your product or services

Just as you can't expect a booming business if you sell mirrors in a country of blinds, you can't expect wrong people to buy your product or service.

A rich bald man will never buy shampoo, even if u r a no.1 sales person or you sell the best product / service.

Do some homework before meeting or calling a new customer . . .

- Is he/she the right person?
- Does he/she have authority of closing the deal?
- Has he/she approached other supplier?
- Is he/she already using such product or service?
- Does he/she qualify for your product?

Do analysis before any approach

Way no. 171 to successful selling

Success breeds success

Celebrate your success as often as you can.

Arranging a get together for your sales team, whenever you achieve a reasonable target, or get a big order, will pass a great wave of positivity in all people around you.

It is a great way to keep up the momentum of sales and maintain high spirit amongst all. Hence it is rightly said that, success attracts more success to your account.

Share your success

Way no. 172 to successful selling

Sincerity and Integrity has a very big impact on your sales

Standing by your customer (new or existing) on timely basis is **sincerity**.

It mainly includes:
- Timely visits and follow ups.
- Addressing his concerns.
- Delivering as promised, and on agreed date.
- On time after sales service

Honesty and being truthful with customers is **integrity**.

It mainly includes:
- Giving correct information
- Being ethical
- Adhering moral principles
- Loyalty

Key important qualities

Way no. 173 to successful selling

Sale Statistics

Some sales statistics which will be helpful:

- 48% of sales people never follow up with a prospect
- 25% of sales people make a second contact and stop
- 12% of sales people only make three contacts and stop
- Only 10% of sales people make more than three contacts
- 2% of sales are made on the first contact
- 3% of sales are made on the second contact
- 5% of sales are made on the third contact
- 10% of sales are made on the forth contact
- 80% of sales are made on the fifth to twelfth contact

Source: Internet

Useful stats

Way no. 174 to successful selling

Make cold calls to people who did not buy from you

Do develop a habit of calling those people who did not buy from you.

Make a call in general chat, asking about their health and wellness of their family members, etc.

Never on a cold call, try to pitch your product/service. Just be calm and do remember that they had turned down your offer last time.

Next time when you are passing from their area/locality, just give a call, 50% people will invite you for tea/coffee, if they are not busy.

But make sure there is reasonable gap between 2 calls.

Do not try to sell on cold calls

Way no. 175 to successful selling

Match the talking speed of customer

Try to match the talking speed of the customer.

If they are talking slowly and at ease, maybe that's what they like, and you should follow the same. By doing so, they will be sure that you understand them clearly. This will help you in building trust.

Use a few words from their previous talks to create more bonding. It shows that you were listening to them carefully and with thorough interest.

People like to be followed, understand this.

Keep pace with customers' speech

Way no. 176 to successful selling

Study your competitors' products / services too

Try to study your competitors' products/services. What are USP's (Unique Selling Prepositions) of their product or service?

If possible, buy their product/service to get a clear and better picture.

If you are not number one, then try to figure out what is it, that is missing in your product or service, which is not letting you go up.

This study will help you in promoting your products/services more efficiently and prepare you well in advance to answer all types of objections.

And you are prepared well in advance to answer all types of objections.

Be knowledgeable

Way no. 177 to successful selling

Customer who does not store your details . . .

People, who do not store your details after meetings / calls, are very unlikely to buy from you. Not bothering to keep your name & number stored with them shows that they will never call you and are not considering you or your product in future.

You should not bank on such customers as following up with them will lead you nowhere but waste in your valuable time.

Understand real customers

Way no. 178 to successful selling

Move step by step towards closing the deal

This is second last stage of the entire sales process (last being after sales service and customer satisfaction).

Closing basically has the following steps:

- Do not get desperate to complete the formalities.
- Be relaxed
- Ask for any last minute suggestions
- Any special requirements which you can fulfill.
- Agreeing on payment terms
- Filling the order form
- Keep emotionally connected
- Take token if order is bigger
- Give acknowledgement receipt
- Assure the date of delivery

Follow basics of closing

Way no. 179 to successful selling

Hand gestures

Do not keep your hands behind your back or inside your pockets. This shows commanding attitude.

In sales, when you do presentations and hand gestures effectively, they convey your message perfectly, leaving a strong impact on your customers' mind. It shows your involvement and interest in the customer and your own product / service.

Hand gestures attracts' attention, adds seriousness and shows emotions to your message that is being conveyed. It advantages you with a non verbal agreement from your customer.

Make effective hand gestures

Way no. 180 to successful selling

Think solutions and not problems

Always think about solutions and you will get solutions. If you think about problems, you will face problems.

When you start thinking on solutions you find different ways to come out of problems. Thinking on solutions will encourage you to automatically overcome obstacles. Look at problems from every angle.
There is absolutely no harm in discussing it with your family & friends. Broadening your audience for solutions is a definite remedy.

Start visualizing solutions in back of your mind in different virtual concepts like diagrams, pictures, etc. Channelize the above concepts efficiently to get the most appropriate solution.

Think solutions

Way no. 181 to successful selling

Exchange as many as business cards as you can

It is good practices to share your profile to people you meet every day and leave your business card in exchange of one.

You never know who may need your service and when? Likewise, you may also require certain services someday.

The best part about a business card is that it is very much convenient and one can preserve it without any hassle.

Easy medium

Way no. 182 to successful selling

Identify the need of customer

This process involves mainly questions and answers. Questions should include fact findings about the customers' expectations, usage, affordability, etc.

But before trying to find out needs, you need to make the customer comfortable to trust you enough. Show friendly and helping approach as a solution provider. Be polite to find out what is going in customers mind. Help him open up slowly.

A smile on your face will be of great help here.
Acknowledge their points.
Why are they looking for such product?
Listen carefully without interrupting. Nodding your head and taking notes while they are speaking will make them feel that you are really concerned.

Build values around customers needs

Way no. 183 to successful selling

Care for customers for autopilot of business

If you truly care for your customer, it will give you the vital ingredient required for your business, i.e., referrals.

If every customer gives you even 2 referrals, your business comes on autopilot mode. You do not need to spend time searching for new clients. The referrals are already half sold people. You just need to give some extra attention to them.

And remember, if you take care of existing customers, you do not even need to ask for referrals, they will send them to you all by themselves.

People will always find you

Way no. 184 to successful selling

You need full confidence in yourself and your product

Be confident in yourself, your selling skills, and furthermore in your product / service.

Now-a-days, people link your confidence with your product / service. They judge your words, your gestures, behavior, etc. before building trust in you.

Even if you have the best product and you do not have confidence, customers will never buy from you.

Confidence can win clients and confidence can sell anything.

Products / services are confidence driven

Way no. 185 to successful selling

Backup plan

Keep a habit of asking yourself questions like,

- What would happen if . . . ?
- Where would I stand if competitors come with new products / services?
- Which strategies shall I apply during tough times in business?
- How would I secure my no. 1 position in market?

You have to be prepared with the answers for the above questions by not relying only on favorable scenarios. Keep back up plans ready for difficult situations in future.

What's your plan 'B'?

Way no. 186 to successful selling

Always listen to prospective customer first

You are always eager to introduce your product, services, qualities, and all such stuff with the opposite person.

Never start your sales talk instantly.

To be more impressive listen to people first.

People love if you show interest in everything they say and then suggest what you can do for them, and how your product or service will help them, if purchased or implemented.

Never use the sentences like—"If you buy this then XYZ will happen". Instead say—"This product will do XYZ for you."

If you listen to customer first, customer will surely listen to you.

Let customer speak

Way no. 187 to successful selling

Give opportunity whenever appropriate

At times you may come across customers who are looking for products / services different from yours'. Due to a your strong relationship with that customer they end up sharing you their requirements of products / services that you do not promote. In such cases do give this opportunity to sales professionals from other field, as this will definitely prove helpful in the long run.

Remember you are always going to be remembered and looked upon with gratitude if you help anyone in their business.

Share opportunities

Way no. 188 to successful selling

Worth of your product / service should be more than the price

Always remember that most of the people bargain for better price before closing the deal.

Inflating the price and then giving discounts is not at all a good practice. Customers also know the average price of your products or services.

So just make them realize that what you are offering is worth more than the price you are asking for.

Increase the worth of your product/service and let people realize that what they are offered is of great value.

To justify worth, you need to talk about the benefits and advantages of your product/service, like durability, good quality, timely after sales service, guarantee, maintenance, etc

Overvalue your product/service

Way no. 189 to successful selling

Show interest in customers' discussion

This can be done through the following techniques:

- Actually listen to them.
- Keeping eye contact.
- Offering some suggestions.
- Asking some relevant questions.
- Asking about their family.
- Include some humour.
- Asking about their business/job.
- Appreciating the theme of office/living room.
- Using words like "that's great" after their sentence is completed.
- Having a friendly approach.
- Guiding them towards sale.

A healthy discussion closes the deal

Way no. 190 to successful selling

Explain each benefit one by one

Explain benefit of your product/service one by one.

Give breather to customer between every explanation. Ask them if they have understood the benefit, then only go for explaining the next benefit.

Make sure you get a nod from the customer to move on to explain the next benefit, and at the end of discussion, the customer has understood all the benefits. And then there are very good chances of closing the sale.

When you explain one by one and take consent on each benefit, the deal is half done.

Go step by step

Way no. 191 to successful selling

Accept suggestions, if better than yours

Listen to every customer carefully. If they are suggesting anything, and if it's better than yours', it's really worth listening.

Your customer may help you with a finest solution because they are the ones who actually use your product / service day in and day out. Considering their opinion upto some extent is definitely going to help in adding value to your business.

When you request your customers for suggestions, they feel valued and are always delighted in every manner.

Suggestion benefit

Way no. 192 to successful selling

Say thanks to people who did not buy from you

You have to thank every customer since he has shared his valuable time with you but also thank them for their genuine reasons of not buying your product / services. Understand your customers and the several reasons for not being able to buy from you.

His feedback will definitely help you make more sales in future and also a chance to gain the same customer who could not buy from you earlier.

Customers may give several reasons like:

- Budget
- Different priorities
- Non availability of choice
- Chosen competitors product//service

Thank you

Way no. 193 to successful selling

Do not hold the line

It happens many a times that the person you are calling may be busy on another call or busy in some other work and cannot take your call at that moment.

The best way is to call later.

Holding the line will drain out your enthusiasm, and half of the things you wanted to discuss will have vanished from your mind.

And, when a person answers your call in such situations, he is still in previous mind frame. He is not totally prepared to listen to you. And it will turn a bad call for you.

Call next time

Way no. 194 to successful selling

Think as if you are self-employed

If you are selling products / services of some company or working for someone, then think as if you are the owner.

What would a owner do to sell his products / services?

Because, if you think as an employed person, The only motive you have, is to achieve sales required just to keep your job, and nothing else. You will not feel like crossing the bars and earning more for the company.

But, if you think as an owner, you will do anything to cross benchmarks. You would work for extra hours, find new strategies, go an extra mile for every possible sale, and so on.

You are self-employed

Way no. 195 to successful selling

See objections as opportunity

See objections as opportunities.

If you are unable to provide an answer to an objection, you are really a bad sales person, and vice versa.

It is another chance given by customer to prove yourself. If you clear his/her objections the sale is for sure.

No matter what ever and how many objections a customer has, you are bound to answer their objections. They are just getting their doubts cleared before buying.

Objection = opportunity

Way no. 196 to successful selling

Stay in touch with customers

As a good sales person you should make sure you stay in touch with your customer at least once in 2 months.

It does not mean you need to call them to show your existence, but you can send your product/service newsletter, new launch, seasonal/birthday/anniversary greetings, thanks giving day, etc . . .

Apart from the above mentioned occasions make sure you call them 3-4 times in a year, just to enquire about if they are happy and satisfied with your product/service they bought. If their answer is 'YES' then ask for referrals or repeat of order.

Be in customers mind

Way no. 197 to successful selling

Carry competitors' data with you

Most amazing technique in today's sales business is to carry your competitor's data with you. If you wish to highlight your product and make your customer compare instantly, add this technique to your sales approach. Convince that your product has more benefits than your competitor, and make your customer consider your product / service accordingly.

Customers are amazed when they see other companies' information with you as they realize that you have saved their time and efforts of searching the information in the market.

Smart sales

Way no. 198 to successful selling

Control yourself

To become a successful sales person you need to control yourself mentally.

Sometimes, meetings take an undesirable and ugly turn. It's mostly in cases of unsatisfied customer.

At these moments, do not use harsh words and abusive tones. It may damage your, as well as your companies image.

Try to control the situation by listening to opposite person politely and once they are through, just say—you will look into the matter personally.

Make sure you figure out the genuineness of anger of that customer, and do solve it if its genuine.

Keep control

Way no. 199 to successful selling

Explain fine prints

Companies have made it a tradition to fine print its terms and conditions in non readable smaller fonts. This advantages the companies as customers ignore to read it because it has many lengthy clauses in smaller fonts. Customers overlook the same and trust your words at the time of closing the deal.

You should be proactive in making your customer aware of such terms and conditions. This will definitely be appreciated and you will be looked upon in pride by all.

Terms and conditions

Way no. 200 to successful selling

A customer never buys a product

Customers do not buy products / services from us. They buy benefits and utilities of our product / service.

Therefore, it's necessary that you are able to explain what your product does, and how it will be helpful to them.

If, your product is going to help your customer in saving time while entering his important data in his computer, then you should educate him on this time saving feature/ benefit, rather than telling him about the coding language and colour scheme options of the software.

Customer buys benefits

Way no. 201 to successful selling

Look for a buoyant market

Find out a buoyant market to place your product/services. You just can't sell anything anywhere.

Study the market well, so you can achieve sales faster. Look where you can sell in more quantities and rapidly.

Always keep on searching new places where you can create demand for your product/service.

Examples:

- "Stationeries" next to schools and colleges
- "Flowers" near temples
- "Food joints" close to commercial complexes
- "Garments shops" in malls

Buoyant market needed

Way no. 202 to successful selling

Document in black and white

The most important aspect of sales is to ensure you document everything on papers in black and white. Take a signed attestation for everything you commit and also for the commitments you receive from others.

This habit will always safeguard you and everyone involved in any particular deal. It acts as a proof and helps to avoid conflicts.

Example:

If, someone takes your position in company, your habit of documenting everything will help the new person to be aware of every customer and their deals.

Maintain evidence

Way no. 203 to successful selling

Do not give unsolicited advice

You have to keep in mind, when your customer is discussing something with someone, on issues not related to you or your business, you should not dare to offer your advice or suggestions. If they are not asking you for your advice, it clearly states that you are not expected to give one.

It may happen unknowingly because of your helpful nature but it amounts to trespassing others domain.
This may make your customer feel offended and spoil your sales.

Note: Never ever give any advice unless asked for.

Maintain distance

Way no. 204 to successful selling

DND

DND means do-not-disturb. It is a facility provided by telephone regulatory authorities to consumers who do not wish to receive solicitation calls from any company / organization for promotions. You also need to include those customers who mention not to be called again.

You need to respect their privacy and make sure to delete those numbers from your database so not a single member from your company ends up calling that particular customer again.

You may have to end up facing legal proceedings if you happen to call customers who have registered for DND.

Adhere to policies

Way no. 205 to successful selling

Nurture competitive spirit

Competitive spirit means the willingness of undertaking every challenge to break your own records. you should have good observation, knowledge about competitors strength and weakness, team work attitude, etc. this will lead to nurture your competitive spirits.

You must share information and ideas that will help you and your team to achieve good sales. Let all be aware of each other's selling skills to obtain maximum results.

Be proactive

Way no. 206 to successful selling

Avoid jargons

Make it easy and understandable for the customer to buy. Using heavy and technical words will turn your prospective away.

Example:

A customer approaches you for buying a computer, and he has only basic knowledge on computers. Hence while explaining him benefits/features use simple language and terminology which he understands, like fast processor, high resolution webcam, high capacity hard disk, etc., instead of jargons like 5.5 GHz, 2000 MHz FSB, 10 GB Internal memory expandable to 20 GB, 1 TB HDD, etc.

Avoiding use of jargons will make customer feel comfortable to take decision to buy instantly.

Jargons hinder sales

Way no. 207 to successful selling

Take control of conversation

Remember, the person who asks more questions, leads the conversation in his way.

By asking question you are making it compulsory for the customer to answer, and then proceed.

The more questions you ask, the more are the chances to win the conversation.

Make sure the questionnaire is related to your product/ service, and should not sound like interrogation.

The more questions you ask, the more you get clearer about the buyers intentions.

Lead with questioning

Way no. 208 to successful selling

Make impressive slides

Proper and skillfully organized slide presentations play a important role in sales process. Some helpful tips while preparing slides are:

- Use graphical representations instead of showing data in table form. It's easy to understand.
- Keep limited words; do not just fill the space.
- Use bullets for explanation.
- Keep limited numbers of slides to justify the presentation.
- Use soothing fonts in dark colors.
- Never use all capitals, unless really necessary.
- Avoid abbreviations and jargons.
- Color combinations should be selected wisely.
- If showing pictures of some article / place, use lively pictures.
- Try to make it self-explanatory.
- Use laser pointer while explaining, rather than obstructing the screen yourself.

Slide show

Way no. 209 to successful selling

Qualities of a buyer

Listed below are some of the qualities of a good prospect which will help you in recognizing one:

- They asks lot of questions
- Tells you what they really needs
- Raises objections and expects clarifications
- Is excited
- Very enthusiastic
- Price is not basic criteria of discussion
- Asks for time to decide
- Shares some personal details without hesitation
- Shows positive gestures
- Gets fully involved in discussion
- Listens to you carefully
- Treats you as a friend
- Is curious to get all details
- Ask you to repeat a few things

Good qualities

Way no. 210 to successful selling

Qualities of a non-buyer

Listed below are some of the qualities of a poor prospect which will help you in recognizing one:

- Keeps quite most of the time
- Does not tell you exactly what he needs
- Has no queries / objections
- Not excited
- Least enthusiastic
- Talks about pricing very often
- Never asks for time to decide
- Hesitates to share personal details
- Shows negative gestures
- Pays partial attention to you
- Pretends to listen
- Treats you as a sales person
- Not so curious to get details
- Never asks you to repeat anything

Poor qualities

Way no. 211 to successful selling

People love getting more of anything

Researches have shown that customers always prefer products / services which have extra benefits.

Examples:

- Extended warranty
- Additional insurance cover
- Personal guarantee

Use this tool to attract sales. It helps you in achieving mass business for your product / services.

Give more to get more

Way no. 212 to successful selling

When someone turns abusive

If someone starts swearing/abusing you because of some reasons known/unknown to you.

Be calm and gently wait till they have blown out all their frustration. Then tell them, if they continue using such unfriendly words, you will be of very little help for them.

It's very much possible that once they have cooled off, they may repent for their words and be embarrassed for their behavior.

Sit and work on solutions to avoid such situation in future.

Remember, no one can keep shouting for more than 2 minutes. After 2 minutes they need a breather. So, take advantage of that breather to suppress their anger.

Handle anger with tactics

Way no. 213 to successful selling

Call backs

It's really necessary to call back the people you meet for business.

Dont wait for them to call you, because they may not. It is your duty to call back, not theirs.

Calling them shows that you really remember and care for them. Moreover, if you do not call them, your competitor will.

Note: Responding within 24 hours is a good practice.

Call backs add value

Way no. 214 to successful selling

Why a salesperson fails?

Reasons for the failure of a salesperson are many, but some common reasons are:

- Lack of courtesy
- Lack of training
- Lack of planning
- Do not take initiative
- No personal goals
- Personal problems
- Do not follow instructions
- No discipline
- Communication problem
- Bad attitude
- Lack of confidence
- Lack of product knowledge
- Lack of enthusiasm
- Lack of ideas and strategies
- Not loyal to customers / company
- Inability to improve

Avoid all of the above

Way no. 215 to successful selling

Non-verbal talks

Around 50% of our communication is non-verbal.

We do not necessarily always talk to convey our point. We use gestures and posture for communication.

A good sales person should learn to read what customers have in their mind, how they are reacting, what are they trying to say/suggest?

Reading a good book on body language will help you a lot to understand non-verbal communication better.

People buy more with their eyes than ears.

Body language

Way no. 216 to successful selling

Have you done what you wanted to do today?

At the end of the day, ask yourself—"Have I done what I wanted to do today?"

Asking this question to yourself will help you a lot.

If you have done all that you were supposed to do in the entire day, then you are on the track. If not, then there is a reason to worry.

Whatever you have not done today, find out the reason, why you could not do it. If there were some unavoidable circumstances (like traffic, client was unavailable, rains, etc) then make it a point to complete that undone activity next day on priority.
If, there are some other unrealistic reasons for not doing things you wanted to do, then you are going off the track, please be focused.

Daily achievements lead to GOALS

Way no. 217 to successful selling

Over confidence kills

Do not ever cheat yourself with overconfidence as it may cost you your career. Being under baseless impression of overcoming everything and portraying that everything is running in your favor is a mere **over confidence**

Avoid overconfidence by . . . .

- Gaining sure knowledge about customers buying motive
- Not giving unrealistic commitments
- Being certain without any study on the issue
- Thinking of overachieving targets during tough times

Be confident

Way no. 218 to successful selling

Take calculated risks

There is risk attached to everything we do in our lives.

Take calculative risks in business and be careful while preparations.

Do consider the following aspects when you find things hazardous in business:

- Finances, emotions, time etc
- Reckless risk
- Avoid impulsive decisions
- Cost cutting
- Utmost use of resources
- Prioritized actions

Taking some sort of risks is necessary for every business growth.

Be prepared and calculative

Way no. 219 to successful selling

If your friends do not buy, no one will buy

If you are unable to sell your product/service to your close friends, then it's really difficult to sell it to others.

Your friends are very close to you, and if you are unable to convince them, then you cannot convince strangers out there.

If known people do not buy, then who will buy?

To gain confidence, start from your friends first.

Sales starts from trusted people

Way no. 220 to successful selling

Reaction vs. response

Reactions are defensive and seem to be disadvantageous, because it makes you uncomfortable with something that is said or done. Reactions are emotionally driven and there is a downside that benefits the opposite person / company. You tend to lose focus and control as reactions offend sentiments and have disparities.

On the contrary, response is more filled with thoughtfulness as it contains logical reasoning. Response is not guided by emotions and includes activeness when acted upon.

You must never react to any situation as it will be advantageous for your competitor.

Respond wisely as it will surely help you achieve good numbers in sales.

Always respond

Way no. 220 to successful selling

Solve others' problems first

If someone gives a reason for not buying your product/service due to some problems and you just walking out from there because they will not buy now, is selfishness.

Instead, try to solve their problem (with their permission), if you think you have some solution.

Discuss the problems and try to help them. This will reveal you care about them. Once their problem is solved, you win their trust and this trust will bring good fortune to you in form of sales.

Help always rewards

Way no. 222 to successful selling

Think what could go right, than wrong

When in crisis or after consecutive failures, we always think what more bad can happen with us. What could go wrong with our product/service?

Actual loss or failure is much less than the fear it creates in our minds.

Always think what could go right, rather than thinking what could go wrong as it will cater ways to find solutions to regain opportunities.

Temporary crisis in business due to unfavorable circumstances / your incorrect decisions is natural phenomenon and thinking how to face it in a right way is essential.

Think right

Way no. 223 to successful selling

There is nothing called— total failure

There is nothing called—total failure. There is always some value in every failure.

A failure may give you a chance to start fresh which will be much better than what you were thinking about previously.

A failure will open up new relations, and opportunity for new exposures which will bring a lot of good experiences

Then, how can there be total failure?

Failure is the best teacher

Way no. 224 to successful selling

A query is not a sale

You should not misunderstand customers if they have approached you with regards to few queries on your product / service as a sale.

Queries do show as if the customer is interested in your product / service, but considering such customer queries as sales is incorrect as it is not a realistic reason.

There are many steps involved from query to sale and in this process around 90% do not get converted in a sale.

This can happen due to several reasons like:

- Window shopping
- Unqualified customer
- Unsuitable product / service for them
- Budget
- Comparing your price / product / service with competitors.

Count actual sales

Way no. 225 to successful selling

Never discus religious, political and personal issues

Since your customers belong to different religions, communities, and favor different political parties, you need to avoid discussions on these topics.

You may hurt someone's sentiments unknowingly, which may permanently ruin your relations.

Avoid yourself falling in such discussions as it may also hurt your own feelings and lead to a conflict if the other person has different opinion on issues discussed.

Respect feelings

Way no. 226 to successful selling

Highlight product on display

Presentation of your product / service plays a very important role for its sales. You need to learn the technique of displaying your product in such a manner that it is self explanatory and attracts customers' attention instantly.

Highlighting your product and making it appealing, is an art to promote your product / service and should be done considering the following aspects:

- Consider it's visibility from everywhere
- Make it glamorous
- Add its benefits in showcase
- Highlight the 'scheme / offers' if applied
- Make it special amongst competitors
- Make it interactive

Display appropriately

Way no. 227 to successful selling

Be humorous

Everyone loves humor in life and just hate people who show dumbness/strictness on their face.

As we all know laughter is the best medicine and it can be used as an add-on quality to become a super sales person.

Tell short incidents/short stories/jokes which make people giggle.

People tend to buy from a happy sales person rather than from a sad face.

Create an enjoyable atmosphere

Way no. 228 to successful selling

Portray your credit

Though it is considered inappropriate, but if done tactfully, will give amazing results. Boosting about yourself and your true achievements in a limited manner will definitely make the customer realize your ability and strengths.

When you tell your customer about how you managed to make business from a well know personality, it makes your customer feel proud about you. This technique needs to be played smartly because it may sound fake if you over do the same.

Example:
It really was an exhausting week; I managed to achieve 200 new accounts for Xyz Company in our bank.

NOTE: It may be risky if not done cautiously.

Smart promotion

Way no. 229 to successful selling

Trade database with trusted salespeople

It is a common practice these days to buy data base for solicitation from external sources to broaden your exposure for the product / services.

You can surely achieve good business by trading this information from variety of channels like:

- Data base vendors
- Sales professionals from other industry
- Trade directories
- Big organizations
- Telephone companies

Note: Please check the company policies if you are working for some company.

Keep increasing your database

Way no. 230 to successful selling

Create an Opening statement

You should create an opening one liner sentence. This should include your introduction, one best quality of your product/service, and its benefits to the buyer.

This line will decide whether the person should listen to you or not.

If your line is good enough, then you have made it half way to the deal.

Examples:

- Good Morning Mr. Mehta, I'm glad to offer you reliable software which will increase your profits by 20% and save your valuable time, I'm sure you will like to know more about it.
- Mrs. Shah I'm excited to meet you for discussing new investment plans, as our bonus offer is assuring you 15% returns just in 1 year with loyalty benefits worth Rs. 10,000/- per lakh.

Punch line

Way no. 231 to successful selling

What is holding you back?

Knowing and improving on your weakest skill will make the largest difference in your sale. To find your weakness you follow few techniques and later accordingly make them your strengths:

- Visit with a colleague to your customer and later take feedback on points you need to work on
- Study your past approaches and presentations to differentiate between the strategies which helped
- If possible, take feedback from non buyers
- Consult your reporting head
- Discuss with your spouse / mentor / close friends

Sharpen yourself

Way no. 232 to successful selling

Sales and Marketing

Sales and marketing is interlinked with each other and is very crucial in today's market for prosperity of your product / services.

In Sales:

You have to apply your ideas to make money. It involves discussion on commercial grounds with the actual buyer with the intention to make sales of our product / service. Sales is more of one-on-one business, your skills fetch profit in real, on making a deal.

In Marketing:

You have to put money to generate sales. Marketing is a process of targeting audience in mass. It is done with an intention to create awareness and curiosity amongst people to buy the product / service. Marketing is a process done prior to sales of the product / service.

Increased revenue

Way no. 233 to successful selling

Give some samples

Give away small samples to prospective customers, so they can have a feel of your product/service.

But make sure you give only small portion as sample, because if they do not buy actual product from you, it's going into charity.

Just let them feel, do not feed them.

Samples

Way no. 234 to successful selling

Do not be scared of competition, just be aware of them

Getting scared about competition can prove fatal for sales of your product / service. Everyone has a right to do business and this should not bother you.

Accepting the fact of variety in product / service and mastering the skill to sell them should be your only motto.

Remember competition is necessary to sharpen your sales skills and improve your product / service.

Competition helps you to be in pace with latest upgrades in your industry and gives you input for research.

Remember market is huge and the demand never ends.

Welcome competition

Way no. 235 to successful selling

Prioritize customers

Divide customers into sure-shots, so-so and just-forget types.

- Sure-shots—there are customers who are sure to buy with minimum efforts. These can be referrals, close friends/relatives, needy people, unsatisfied customers of your competitors, etc.

- So-so—these are customers who may buy with maximum efforts. These are doubtful customers.

- Just-forget—you do not need to waste time with them. Whatever you do, they will never buy from you.

Priority

Way no. 236 to successful selling

Only sell your product/ service, all the time

Always MIND YOUR OWN BUSINESS.

Sometimes we come across a different class of people, who listen to you as obligation with some other idea in their mind. They will ask you to help them promote their product/service/idea in exchange they will promise buying your product.

There are very good chances that such people will not buy from you once their work is done.

Ask such people to buy your product/service first and then think about helping them without going out of the way. Do not let your business affect negatively.

You are here to do your business, not others. Just think . . . Will anyone do your business leaving theirs' aside?

Help others without compromising on your business

Way no. 237 to successful selling

Clarify questions / objections / doubts

Unless and until you clarify all doubts/questions/ objections of a customer, they won't buy.

Take objections as next step towards closing. You seem to be more promising when you answer your customers' objections as they want more and more information about your product / service.

Your sharp knowledge and your way to educate your customer about your product / service, lowers your customers hesitation for not buying.

Clarify objections

Way no. 238 to successful selling

Some common terms used in sales

Advertising	Benefit
Brand	Bulk
Business to business	Business to customer
Closing	Commission
Concession	Database
Decision	Demo
Exclusive	Features
Finance	Guarantee
Incentive	Lead
Margin	Marketing
Payments	Price
Quality	Quantity
Rapport	Relationship
Service	Standard
USP	Value

General stipulations

Way no. 239 to successful selling

Become a sales magnet

We all are human magnets who constantly attract alike people. We comprehend similar quality individuals and create an influence on them.

Likewise implement such magnetic qualities that will attract customers only to you and increase their interest in you. You need to create such an impact that they should always be eager to meet and hear from you.

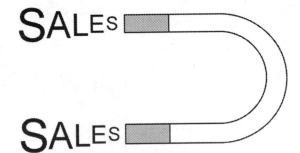

Be magnetic

Way no. 240 to successful selling

Think you are the first sales person meeting them

Customers may have heard from many of your competitors before, but have not heard from you. Do not worry, if they already know about the product / service, because they have seen other sales people prior to you.

You have to be determined enough about your product / service. The only aspect that you need to make your customer believe is that how your product / service and its benefits are different from others.

Keeping the above things in mind, will make you feel that you are the 1st sales person meeting your customer.

Be new for everyone

Way no. 241 to successful selling

Do not take impulsive decisions

Impulsive decision majorly relates to unskilled management and unplanned activities, leading an organizational collapse.

Avoid impulsive decisions not only in profession but also in personal life.

Impulsive decision originates:

- Unbalanced performance
- Bad reputation
- Wrong decision
- Financial loss
- Mental agony

Do not act in hurry

Way no. 242 to successful selling

Make people say "Yes" in conversations

Learn the technique of asking people questions, which has sure shot "Yes" answers.

If you ask such questions:

What a pleasant day today, isn't it?
I am sure you like the product sir?
Sir I am sure money is not an issue, but time is an issue with big people like you?
Madam would be so happy if you choose to buy this?

Most of the people will answer in "Yes" for above questions.

The more "YES's" you hear the closer you are to hear a "YES" for the deal too.

Make people say more "YES's"

Way no. 243 to successful selling

Transparency is important

Do not ever hide anything from customers; it will cost you your career. You have to maintain transparency under every circumstance for sustaining in the industry forever.

Everything you do in life is on the basis of trust on something/ someone, the moment you find that things are not transparent enough you tend to back out from the situation. Similarly when you hide anything from your customer and when it is noticed, it brings a dead end to everything you have achieved in past.

Be transparent

Way no. 244 to successful selling

Understand the difference between COST and PRICE

Though cost and price are 2 different words, but many a times it is understood as same. These 2 words mean different in buyers and sellers perceptive.

For sellers:
"Cost" is the amount incurred while producing the product / service. and "price" is the amount that they sells the product / service for.
The difference between the above is his gross profit.

For buyers:
"Price" is the amount that they initially pay for purchase of the product / service. "Cost" is the amount that they incur to maintain the product / service to enjoy the full benefits till its existence.

Cost differs than price

Way no. 245 to successful selling

Do not sound fake on calls

Do not show over friendliness on phone. It will not help you at all.

Be gentle, polite and sound genuine.

Control tempo of your speech. Do not be too fast (your call will be disconnected), do not be too slow (opposite person does not have that much of time for you). Speak neither too fast nor too slow, just maintain the speed which you maintain during a conversation, in general.

Speak pleasantly

Way no. 246 to successful selling

Take the challenging path, you may strike gold

Whenever you need to choose between 2 ways, choose the challenging way.

Less travelled roads give you more experience and many new things are learnt and experienced on this way.

Be different to get different. If you follow the crowd you will be just one of them, but if you go against the crowd, you may find what no one has found.

Remember Christopher Columbus? He took a very challenging path and got recognition.

Challenges reward

Way no. 247 to successful selling

Offer less choice

If you offer limited choice to a customer, your customer is not confused and decision making becomes easy.

On the contrary, if you offer variety (2 and more) of products to your customer, they tend to feel that if they opt or chose to buy xyz product from the variety offered, they may miss on the others. Such confusion leads them to postpone their decision or they may not buy anything at all.

Instead analyze your customers' potential and accordingly offer your products to them.

Offer smartly

Way no. 248 to successful selling

Use presentation materials only for support

Never depend on presentation materials too much. These are meant for your support only. You need to explain your product to customers yourself. A sale is difficult just by showing power point presentation or distributing broachers in a meeting.

You need to understand that it's not only the presentation material that sells your product, but indeed those are your presentation skills which help the customer to take the decision.

It is a wise advice to give away broachers/leaflets at the end of the meeting, after you have completed your presentation. People get distracted if you distribute them before or during presentation, as their attention is focused on what you are talking and what is in the broucher. They start searching for pages/points/pictures/diagrams that you are explaining.

Presentation material is secondary

Way no. 249 to successful selling

Speak to customers just as you speak with family and friends

It matters a lot when you maintain a friendly tone with your customers as you do within your family and friends. It makes the other person feel comfortable and open for conversation.

You get customers genuine feedback as they do not hesitate to share their views personaly. Your friendly approach builds up a bonding and your sales figure improves in the long run.

In sales, word of mouth plays a very important role. Hence your communication on personal level helps you master in the sales industry.

Communicate for bonding

Way no. 250 to successful selling

Do not use customers in example

We often tend to give examples during discussion with our customers. Ensure you do not use customer or their loved once in the example as you may accidently end up insulting them. Your customer will get offended if you mistakenly do so.

Your attentiveness is very important while giving such examples and you should include non existing members like xyz person etc . . . as this will prove that you are a wise sales professional who understands to the need of proper explanation with good use of examples.

Sales examples are made up stories to attract business, hence before reciting should be practiced properly.

Use examples wisely

Way no. 251 to successful selling

Know when to be silent

Though all sales people like to talk, as it is their valued selling tool, but learning when to be silent is also worth knowing.

Keep silence for a few seconds after you complete your sentence, which makes the opposite person feel respected, as you are giving him time for his response. And he gets more time to answer, rather than just saying Yes/No.

By doing so, you force a person to respond, especially people who do not come up with their answers quickly.

Silence speaks for itself

Way no. 252 to successful selling

Selling in exhibitions and alike

Do not just distribute broucher / leaflet to people passing by your stall, because these will surely end up in bins.

Instead welcome people upto the product. Explain them; allow them to physically touch the product. They should feel it to buy it.

If the customer shows interest ask for his contacts details or visiting card and then give him the broucher. Call these people within next 2-3 days for appointments.

Remember the person who hesitates in giving you his contact details etc, is really not a buyer of your product/ service

Exhibition etiquettes

Way no. 253 to successful selling

Never use these statements

You should strictly avoid using the following statements as it will surely risk your sales:

- "I do not know" instead say "I'll check the information for you very soon."

- "I'm not sure" instead say "Let me confirm this for you"

- "I'll consider it" instead say "I will add this as suggestion from you"

- "I'll get back to you" instead say "Can I revert back in . . . . time"

- "I am not responsible for . . ." instead say "Let me see what best I can do"

Save your sales

Way no. 254 to successful selling

Pearls of wisdom

Pearls of wisdom means sayings, statements, punch lines, famous quotes, phrases etc from personalities within our culture.

Everybody enjoys' hearing and using them in their daily conversations. Pearls of wisdom shorten the explanation, tackle complex issues and convey with ease.

Sales professionals should use this powerful tool, as it helps you to win the conversation.

Examples:

- Anyone who has never made a mistake, has never tried anything new—Albert Einstein

- It takes time to be a success, but time is all it takes.—Socrates

- What we think we become.—Buddha

Strengthens your point of view

Way no. 255 to successful selling

Do not mention designation on business card

People rarely store business cards of sales professionals and avoid relations with sales people because they fear of getting unwanted approaches / solicitations for their products / services.

Avoiding designation on business cards of sales professionals or replacing them as 'Relationship manager', 'business development manager' etc. As it is the new flair to strike customers and maintain your business of sales.

New way

Way no. 256 to successful selling

Prepare for every sales call

Prepare yourself before every sales call. Keep all the information handy which you may require to share with the opposite person.

If possible, briefly study about the person or his company whom you are going to call. Do practice calling his name, if it is a difficult one. Because, people do not like their names to be pronounced wrongly.

Do keep in mind the purpose of the call and for how long you should be taking other persons valuable time.

Ensure that your every call sounds like the first call of the day.

Perfect calling

Way no. 257 to successful selling

Go prepared . . . . make a checklist

Do not ever go un-prepared for any meeting.

Carry all the documents, right from presentation catalogue, benefits, costing, working, timeline, delivery, maintenance plan, after sales details, to order confirmation form and payment receipt.

Carry all that is required for a full cycle of perfect sales.

If you forget any one of these, it's a bad show, and may hinder / delay the sale.

Make a checklist

Way no. 258 to successful selling

Scrutinize unusual order

Whenever you get an unusual order, scrutinize it thoroughly. Because, unusual things only cause unusual profit or unusual loss. If its profit then fine, but what if it transforms into loss?

The order can be from some unknown person who was not in your client list, or an unrealistic bulk order.

Check the worthiness of order and then proceed cautiously.

Example:

Someone may call you for bulk purchase against cash on delivery terms, please consider its authenticity and accordingly process the delivery or you may end up a loss in transit.

Authenticity

Way no. 259 to successful selling

Suspect and Prospect

Suspect is someone who you think can buy from you. He may be in need of your product, and he may become your prospect.

Prospect is someone who has a specific need and could buy from you.

Always be in search of a suspect. It's not a 10 am to 5 pm business; it's a full time business.

All suspects are not prospects

Way no. 260 to successful selling

Get emotionally connected

Get connected to your customer emotionally.

The best way to get connected emotionally is to send greetings on their birthdays, anniversaries, etc.

New Year and seasonal greetings have become common now a days, anyone hardly reads them, because they come in bulk.

But when you send birthday/anniversary greetings it touches their hearts, as its only sent by loved ones.
This activity will always make them feel cared and you will create a greater bonding in the long run.

Emotional contact is the easiest way for sales.

Remember birthday/anniversary

Way no. 261 to successful selling

Thoughtful recommendations

Everyone likes to recommend and get recommendations.

Thoughtful recommendations add value to your relationship.

While recommending something to customers, please do consider their:

Status
Spending habits
Family
Requirements
Benefit

Note: Ensure taking permission before give recommendations.

Communicate for bonding

Way no. 262 to successful selling

Think from the goal

A very important aspect for every sales professional are his targets.

"Thinking from the goal" is the new trend that needs to be considered by sales individuals to get optimum consistency in achieving their targets.

To be more precise, when you think FROM THE GOAL, you see yourself as successful professional in sales. You start visualizing how you achieved your targets on schedule; you see your actual progress and automatically design yourself by jotting down the steps on paper.

This method also helps you to see barriers / problems that could affect your targets, ultimately making you equipped with a solution in time.

Visualize goal

Way no. 263 to successful selling

Remember your bad sales

Bad sales always teach you a lesson and you must remember it forever. Many a times in pressure to close a deal you may mistakenly over promise a customer or end up giving wrong information with regards to your product and services, which later results in a bad sale that adds to customers frustration.

Consider such instances' of bad sales as learning lessons and ensure you do not let such sales happen again.

Bad sale is a good teacher

Way no. 264 to successful selling

Leave extra order forms / broucher / leaflets

Asking for references is a time consuming process.

As you cannot ask your customer for references until he is satisfied with your product / service, and it will need follow-ups too for getting 2-3 references. The customer may be busy, or he may ignore you once purchase is done.

But leaving some extra order forms, broachers, leaflets, etc., will force them to share the material with his friends, relatives and colleagues.

Response rate is quite high in such cases.

Note: The customer will never ask for extra promotion material. You need to take the initiative, and ask them to share it with other interested parties.

Shortcut to new customer's walk-ins

Way no. 265 to successful selling

Be a positive thinker

Positive thinking always brings positive results.

Just think what happens whenever you get a positive thought in your mind . . . . all of a sudden you are charged with positive mood, and your confidence goes up, and you become optimistic.

One positive thought starts the series of hundreds of positive thoughts.

Be +ive

Think positive

Way no. 266 to successful selling

Dress/ talk in accordance of region

You will not connect to your customer if there is a difference in your approach (dressing and talks) as per his region. This difference will keep you away from initiating any relation with them.

You need to dress up relatively and present your product as per his way of communication. This builds up emotional bonding with your customer and they tend to accept you for your interest.

Example:

If you wish to sell a tractor to a farmer and you approach him at his farms in a business suit with foreign vocabulary, it is definitely not going to give you any benefit, instead approach them in their locally accepted manner.
Hence a proper approach is needed to establish a bonding with your customer.

Keep regional approach

Way no. 267 to successful selling

What drives sales?

Benefits	Excitement	Pleasure
Choice	Features	Praise
Companionship	Freedom	Prestige
Consistency	Happiness	Protection
Convenience	Hobby	Recognition
Demand	Hygiene	Reputation
Ease	Influence	Respect
Ego	Leisure	Stability
Enjoyment	Passion	Style
Entertainment	Peace of mind	Value

Sales drivers

Way no. 268 to successful selling

Do not discuss your product / service in detail over the phone

Never get into practice of discussing product/service in detail over the phone. Take appointment for a meeting, or if the customer is too busy for a meeting, then send him details through email, or courier.

Discussing on a call looks like a loose talk, and it's really not possible to give the actual understanding of product/service on a call.

Once the customer is aware of your product/service, then only closing on call is possible.

Meet personaly

Way no. 269 to successful selling

Ask for testimonial letter from satisfied customers

A testimonial letter is the living proof of your achievements with great satisfactions.

These are powerful tools which will build your rapport in advance with new customers. People are 50% sold if they go through testimonial letters written/signed by big shots and famous personalities.

Use these testimonial letters on your company's website, on company advertising material etc as this will always favor your business in making good sales.

Testimonial letter

Way no. 270 to successful selling

Conversion ratio

Conversion in business means the difference of actual paying customers amongst the inquiries made for the xyz product / service. It is maintained in a form of ratio to analyze the actual business made by the product/ service against its actual inquiries made.

You have to understand this conversion ratio by studying your sales reports which will result in clear idea about the status of your work. It helps you to understand your best market and in increasing your focus more effectively.

You can start working more efficiently ones you know your conversion ratio.

$$\text{Conversion Ratio} = \frac{\text{Number of closings}}{\text{Number of inquiries}}$$

Helps in sales analyses

Way no. 271 to successful selling

SWOT Analysis

This is the best way to evaluate **S**trength, **W**eaknesses, **O**pportunities and **T**hreats of your product / service. Writing down all the factors affecting the above 4 elements in a table form will help you.

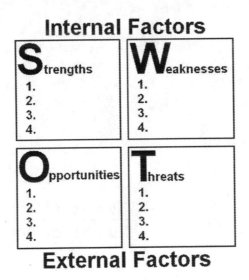

SWOT

Way no. 272 to successful selling

Do not give up follow ups

Do not stop follow ups just because customer said NO on the very first approach.

Studies have shown that it takes atleast 4-5 calls/meeting to actually close the sale.

So do not expect to close on first call/meeting, it is not normal.

Their 'No' can simply mean they are not ready to buy now. So, give some more knowledge about your product/service which will be helpful in getting a 'Yes'.

Have you bought anything on first sales call/meeting?

But remember to follow politely without irritating the opposite person.

Follow until you hear "NO"

Way no. 273 to successful selling

Write down points in meeting

It shows that you are attentive in listening to customers and taking their points/words seriously.

It shows them your good intentions for genuine sales.

It helps you remember all the points of discussions. Otherwise you may forget a few points, which could have been important for sales.

Note points

Way no. 274 to successful selling

Make a list of benefits of your product/service

The best way to win your customers confidence is by being prepared with the list of benefits of your product / service.

Majority of times, some of the common objections are answered upfront by informing the benefits as it instantly connects your customer with your product / service.

Customers start visualizing how your product / service is going to benefit them.

Approaching customers with the list of benefits always adds to a smooth sale and saves your efforts and time.

Benefits sale

Way no. 275 to successful selling

Conclude call/meeting on good note

Practice ending every call/meeting with a good note. Do not just hang up or get up and walk away, if the customer did not listen to you or it was a bad call over the phone. Be polite to say—thank you for giving your valuable time, and have a really good day sir/mam.

People will remember you.

Note: It is a good practice to send a thank you card after the meeting.

Make everyone's day

Way no. 276 to successful selling

Repeat what works

Every product has an advantage of good sales through a particular channel or medium. These channels always deliver optimum results when acted upon.

Examples:

- A garment company has to make sales to the end-users through retailers in market. These companies approach retailers in market for selling their product.
- A sales person from real estate industry who gets good business from a particular medium i.e. brokers, should practice and repeat the method by appointing maximum brokers to his network.

The above examples state that one should repeat the method that works the best for their sales.

Repeat to grow

Way no. 277 to successful selling

Barter game

Giving away gifts affects your sales a lot.

It can be a sample of your product/service or some other thing which people will easily accept without any hesitation.

And by accepting gift people become a sort of liable to buy from you. Just as the saying "you have taken something from me, now I want something from you too".

It's a selfish way of asking for deals, but it really works.

You give and you get

Way no. 278 to successful selling

Discounts and concessions harmful in sales

Do not give discounts / concessions easily. It should be the last resort for difficult sale.

Moreover, customers think that you had offered them inflated price earlier and later you offer discounts / concessions to the close the sale, hence leading to a bad sale.

Talking about discounts and concessions will affect your sales unfavorably, because those customers will start spreading negativity in market and will also degrade your product / service.

Avoiding discounts / concessions will always sustain your brand name and add to profits in the long run.

Example:

A renowned jewellers do not give discounts but do offer flexibility in payment terms and promise benefits on next purchase.

No discounts / concessions

Way no. 279 to successful selling

Make eye contacts

Establish eye contact, without staring into customers' eye. It proves that you are listening to them and are in tune with them. It shows your presence and thought process.

Benefits of eye contact:
- Better confidence
- Shows authority
- Makes customer comfortable
- Reduces public speaking fear
- Builds trust

Interpret with eyes

Way no. 280 to successful selling

Think about next 5 sales

Whenever you are closing a sale, start thinking about your next 5 sales.

How are you going to close next 5 sales?
Are there any in pipeline?
Has any customer committed any sure shot buy?
Or do you need to start from the very first sales call?

Always keep next sales ready to be executed. There should not be any major gap in 2 consecutive sales as it will start adding to tension in business.

You should maintain the chain of making consecutive sales every time because it will boost yours and teams capacities in achieving good business.

Keep up the sales rhythm

Way no. 281 to successful selling

Never regret

Learn not to regret. It's just a waste of your valuable time, thinking on something which has happened and cannot be changed.

Put that energy and talent on thinking what is to be done to avoid such situations, and move ahead.

Regretting invites the following common problems:

- Depression
- Loss of concentration
- Adds to irritation
- Loss of confidence
- Affects performance

Do not be sorry

Way no. 282 to successful selling

Take help from others

Asking for help should not make you feel inferior or a looser. People are always willing to help someone in trouble.

If someone asks you for some help, aren't you eager to help him/her? Yes we do :).

It's just that you are unable to solve the problem at this moment, and want to take advice from some experienced / knowledgeable person.

Taking help and suggestions before taking a decision helps us avoid mistakes and gives us an opportunity to learn from others experience without any cost.

Asking for a valid and reasonable help to improve productivity and creativeness is always recommended as it benefits you in avoiding mistakes.

People love to help

Way no. 283 to successful selling

Attempt trial close

This step is necessary to check whether customer is in agreement with you or not. Such checks help you to understand when to give more input or let go a client.

Trial close is a questioning process to verify the interest of customer in your product / service. The purpose of your questioning should be to get a YES from them. If you get a NO, then there are still some objections which are to be answered before trying a close.

And if, the customer closes the deal in your trial close then you save time too.

Trial close saves time

Way no. 284 to successful selling

Backup important data

Make sure you keep backup of all your important data atleast at two different locations and in 2 different mediums.

Due to vastness in todays work culture, everything has to be on papers i.e. written in black and white.

Hence it is essential you maintain data at 2 different locations, because if your softcopy gets corrupted, you have hard copy in place and vice versa.

Taking backup at regular intervals for your important documents & contacts is very essential as it helps you to safeguard your data from any unwanted calamities.

Backup can be maintained in several ways like Pen drives, hard disk, emails, servers etc.

Keep backup

Way no. 285 to successful selling

Set high standards for yourself

Setting high goals is necessary to keep you up float in today's competitive market. Your high standards contribute to your achievements, credibility and market value.

Benefits of setting high standards are:

- Aggression towards work
- High self esteem
- Improved decision making
- Influential

Set high standards for yourself, and break your own records.

Set high standards

Way no. 286 to successful selling

Selling is caring

Your focus should be on customers 'needs' and you need to help them in achieving it. When you care for their needs, sales takes place automatically.

Remember that your customer is someone who will rate you for your approach & guidance. They will always recollect you and your commitments with regards to your products / services.

Always remember that the customer is entertaining you with his valuable time just because he needs the right solution from you and the use of your product / services. It is an emotional connection between you and your customer that comes into existence due to your product/ service.

If you feel something is good for them, you share frankly & if not, still do the same. Customers appreciate honesty.

"You care" attitude

Way no. 287 to successful selling

Do not fix first meeting in hotel/restaurant

Make sure you fix your first meeting in office (yours or customers').

Do not ever fix your first meeting in any hotel or restaurant; it's very much likely that you will end up paying bills for not so sure deal.

It's worth once in a while when the client is not from local city, and has come all the way to see you. Or if you are far from your office, then greet your customer in some restaurant / hotel as you get a chance to show hospitality and the possibility of closing deal is improved.

Spend only if required

Way no. 288 to successful selling

After sales service

Giving a good after sales service is very important, because it will decide your future sales and rapport.

After sales service is an investment which needs to be nurtured properly.

Essential points to be considered in after sales service:

- Attending timely with perfect solutions
- Billing fairly for any repairs / upgrades
- Feedbacks on repairs

Advantages of after sales service:

- Consistent business
- Customer satisfaction
- Brand loyalty

Good after sales service is a must

Way no. 289 to successful selling

Cross sale your products/ services immediately

Cross selling means selling related product/service to your actual sold product/service.

Like, if you are selling mobiles, then surely you can sell SIM, anti-virus, talk time, scratch guard, pouch/cover, car charger, etc with the mobile you just sold.

Its business, because anyways the customer is going to buy these things today or tomorrow from somewhere, then why not from you right now?

Cross selling

Way no. 290 to successful selling

What influences buying?

Basically, 2 things contribute to any buying decision, and these are:

<u>Personal Cause:</u> customer has some basic requirements and needs to buy. These are the primary requirements for living (food, cloths, house, etc)

<u>Social Cause:</u> Customer needs to adjust and upgrade himself in culture, society, friend circle, etc. and wants to enjoy life like others, and it becomes necessary to buy (car, farm house, jwellery, etc).

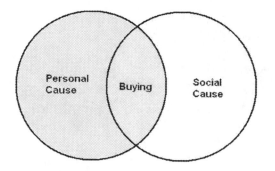

Buying causes

Way no. 291 to successful selling

1st objection is mostly a false objection

It is very common that every customer comes with objection to avoid sales person. You need to understand that every 1st objection raised by customers is always a false objection and you need to tackle it cleverly.

Examples of false objections:

- I am busy
- Too costly
- Out of budget
- Shortage of space
- Not my choice
- Not required
- Not now
- I already have it

Do not buy 1st objection

Way no. 292 to successful selling

Do not criticize or complain

Do not ever criticize or complain about your competitors or their products/services.

It may damage their image and also your reputation.

You will be looked upon as a criticizer.

Instead, talk about advantages of your product/service, so people tend to buy from you.

People who criticize or complaint are regarded as unprofessional & not welcomed. Such unethical behavior will surely spoil your future in any industry you work for.

Note: Do not criticize people, criticize their ideas.

No one is bad

Way no. 293 to successful selling

Leave an order form

This situation is not new to any sales person, when people say they cannot take decision now, and ask for time, or even they hold / reject the proposal.

In such situation, rather than just walking out, you should make a practice of leaving a filled order form with self-addressed envelope or your contact details written on reverse of the order form.

There are good chances that the customer gets back to you after a few days.

It really works

Way no. 294 to successful selling

When self-doubt creeps in your mind

Whenever you feel dull and confidence level is low, self doubt makes its way into your mind.

To face such situations, just rewind your good memories.

- See what you have achieved in good times.
- How that great idea entered your mind and you convinced your boss?
- How you made those mind-boggling sales and received appreciation from all?

Just think of performing the same way again.

And you will gain confidence instantly to make a fresh start.

Rewind memories

Way no. 295 to successful selling

Quick sales rarely happen

At times you may come across a very easy sale that happened in a short time. It may have happened due to several reasons like:

- Customer was keen on buying
- Reference sale
- Promotional offer

Such sales do not take place in routine, so should not be counted as a daily business. Though they add profits but happen once in a while. A good sales professional adds variety of channels to make sales in other possible ways.

Quick sales = limited business

Way no. 296 to successful selling

Handle all types of customers

Handling customers from different professions is always recommended as it sharpens your skills to perform better.

Attending a normal customer is something that will maintain you at a common platform and limit performance, on the contrary when you meet tough customers who are well established professionals in their industry, it always give you scope to excel and exposure to activities that help you win their interests.

Such practice always proves beneficial as it keeps you prepared and confident to be called as a experienced sales professional.

Consider variety in customers

Way no. 297 to successful selling

Join some social club

A social club is the best place to get connected with new faces and getting referrals.

Make yourself a active member there. It will make you visible.

You can build good rapport with people first and slowly push your product/services into their mind.

It is the fastest way to make rocket sales and get recognized.

Join club

Way no. 298 to successful selling

Ask for only 2 referrals at a time

Whenever you have a satisfied customer, ask for 2 referrals immediately.

Do not ask for whole list of his friends. It sounds selfish, rude and unethical.

First work on these 2 referrals because the customer has given you these referrals after going through his list and considered only those people who he thinks might buy from you.

If it works, then ask for 2 more referrals from him/her.

If his referrals do not work, then it's not worth asking for more from the same customer, as he / she may not be having actual referrals for your business and you might waste your time.

Start with only 2 referrals

Way no. 299 to successful selling

Use good quality sales material for presentation

Good quality sales material for presentation is necessary for impactful endorsement of your product / service.

Good quality sales material helps you in:

- Showcasing worth of your product / service
- Business status
- Product prominence
- Appealing
- Curiosity
- Makes the other person feel valued
- Live feel

Impressive sales material is a must

Way no. 300 to successful selling

Answer all calls with enthusiasm / excitement

Answer all calls with enthusiasm and excitement. As if you are waiting for the whole day for this particular person to call.

Standup and talk for better command on conversation. Believe me, it really helps.

Your excitement is transferred to the caller, making him feel good and he likes this welcoming gesture, and he is more likely to open for discussion on friendly level.

Every call that you make, should sound like your first call of the day, filled with enormous enthusiasm.

Be excited on calls

Way no. 301 to successful selling

Be focused on buyers, and not on money

When you focus on making money through sales, you forget the buyer.

If your intention of closing the deal is only money, then you will start force selling and become selfish.

But, on the other hand, if your intentions are to give the buyer the best benefits, the best service, best satisfaction, best trustworthiness, and then you become a true successful sales person in life.

Help people get what they want, and you will get what you want.

Be customer oriented

Way no. 302 to successful selling

Seasonal businesses needs special planning

There are certain businesses that have limitations depending on favorable seasons.

For example:

- Construction business is sluggish during monsoon.
- Pesticides make high revenue in monsoon
- Tourism industry grows during vacation

You need to consider the fact of seasonal sales & accordingly act to average out your income for the year.

Your planning should include ideal strategies and if you fail to do so, you have to wait until next favorable conditions for your business.

Seasonal sales

Way no. 303 to successful selling

Give options for meeting

Be blunt in asking whether the opposite person is free at 10:00 am or 4:00 pm / Tuesday or Friday for meeting. It will leave him with no choice than choosing one.

When you offer options for meeting, it will force the customer to give you one and when you do not approach them with the option, customer takes the advantage of saying 'NO'.

10:00 AM or 4:00 PM

Tuesday or Friday

Ask which; among the 2?

Way no. 304 to successful selling

Word of mouth works the best

Word of mouth publicity works the best even today.

When advertising, you come across new people. Which is much more time and money consuming.

But in word to mouth publicity, your rapport is built on its own. When you give the best service to your customers, they talk about your product/services to their friends/relatives. They want their closed ones to have same satisfaction as they gained from you and your product/service.

All these people advertise for you freely. They are your advocates.

And the customers who are referred to you from this publicity are already half sold.

Word of mouth

Way no. 305 to successful selling

Create a need for your product/service

People just do not purchase because they have money. But they purchase if it's really needed.

So create a need for your product/service which people cannot reject. Such a need, that they cannot resists your product/service. Make them realize that what you are suggesting them is really needed.

You can achieve this by sharing benefits / features of your product/service and how their life will change after buying it.

Create need

Way no. 306 to successful selling

Give special attention to big / corporate customers

Big corporate and bulk order placing companies are back bone of your business. Do give special attention to them.

These customers do not like to get neglected. Your negligence means total loss of business with them.

Do meet them time to time and maintain your rapport for a long lasting business.

Remember, you need them more than they need you or your product/service. You have to keep them happy and satisfied all the time as referrals from these people will bring booming sales to your business.

Deal wisely

Way no. 307 to successful selling

Be Positive in your thoughts and deals

It takes the same efforts to think positive or negative. So why not put all your energy in thinking only positive thoughts.

Your desire to sell should be more than the fear of getting rejected.

Positive thoughts lead you in several ways:

- Boost enthusiasm
- Brings you close to the deal
- You become optimistic
- Attitude and approach
- Leads you to series of positivity
- Keeps you on toes

Think positive

Way no. 308 to successful selling

Appreciate every single person involved with you

Make sure you appreciate every single person involved with you in making your sales complete. You could not have done it alone. Make people feel important and pat them for being with you. They will feel motivated, and all this will count in good future relations and sales.

When you include your team in achievements they feel provoked of performing better resulting increase in sales figures.

One must maintain this understanding that every achievement made by the individual involves team effort and by appreciating the same you pass positivity amongst all.

Appreciate people for their presence

Way no. 309 to successful selling

Become good observer

The key to be a master in sales is to be a very good observer. Your observation about everything around you should be very strong and accurate.

Pay close attention to everything around you in such a way that you recollect things whenever you need them.

- To become a good observer you need to grasp maximum information around you.
- Stay updated with news related to your business

This will prove significant for your career and for your life as a whole.

Improve observation

Way no. 310 to successful selling

When customers have price objection

When people say that your price is too high, it could mean several of the following:

- They cannot afford it
- Its costlier than they thought
- They are expecting you to lower the price
- They expect some add-on benefits
- They are not the decision makers
- Your competitor is offering at less
- They want to close the discussion and stop from any further sales approach.
- They are just collecting data from different vendors, and want to research before buying.
- They have changed their mind for buying.
- Product / service seem to be unjustified in their eyes

Analyze and approach

Way no. 311 to successful selling

Do not expect customer to fill forms

If there is lot of form filling involved in your closing process, then please help your customer in this process. People just hate the writing part.

You can just ask them to fill the important points and do the rest form filling yourself. But make sure you show them the filled form before processing.

Please do not insist customers to put signatures on half filled order forms.

Sales formality

Way no. 312 to successful selling

Your y-o-y growth should be more than market growth

If you are an organic food supplier, and organic food market grows by 10% per year then your growth should be more than 10% to reap good profits.

Knowledge of market growth is very much essential to be in good shape. It helps in understanding your company's growth. You will have to frame your strategies according to the growth rate.

Example

If you invest in shares, market has grown 20% in 1 year, and if your returns on investments are above 20%, then you have outperformed the market, but if it is less than 20% then there is a reason to worry.

Grow more than your market

Way no. 313 to successful selling

Make customer a family

A customer builds confidence and trust in you before they opt to buy your product/ service.

It is very healthy to maintain that bonding forever by treating them as family members. This will always cherish you with a feeling of achievement in true sense. Welcome their views for your personal decisions in life, upto some extent.

Your affection for the customer will always be perceived and they will certainly value you forever.

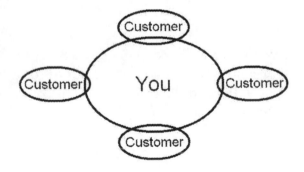

We are a family

Way no. 314 to successful selling

Intuitions are bigger than your beliefs

Take support of your intuitions. Listen to your inner self. Sometimes intuitions are more powerful than your beliefs.

Ask yourself question and listen to the first answer that comes to your mind. You must have noted, if you are doing something wrong, you feel uneasy. Such feelings cannot be expressed in words but can be sensed as butterfly feeling.

Learn to take help from your intuitions to avoid wrong decisions.

Intuitions also help you in taking wise decisions.

Intuitions = early signals

Way no. 315 to successful selling

Sales is a 24 hour business

Be available for your customers 24x7.

Even if it's a holiday, or you have just returned from a overly exhaustive meeting/journey, just attend the customer.

I am not recommending you to travel at odd hours to give service, just asking to take note of customers concern at any hours.
If you don't, then your competitors will.

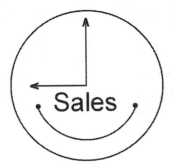

24x7 service

Way no. 316 to successful selling

Learn 5 new words everyday

Learn 5 new words every day. Understand its meaning and try to use them in daily conversation.

Having a good vocabulary will help you a lot in your selling business. Do not fall short of good and impressive words in discussions. As far as possible use exact words than substitute words.

Reading, writing, solving puzzles, playing scrabble, scanning dictionary for new words, etc. will improve your vocabulary and word power.

If you learn 5 new words every day, it counts to 1,825 words a year, and 9,125 words in 5 years. Can you imagine what skills of communication you will gather in 2-5 years?

Words power = sales power

Way no. 317 to successful selling

Do not push your business card

Do not push your business card as soon as you meet a customer.

A small introduction is expected prior to exchanging business cards.

You should always create an urge for yourself in customers' mind. Let him take the opportunity to ask for a business card from you.

Hint: The customers, who do not ask for a business card, are not serious buyers.

Value your business card

Way no. 318 to successful selling

Believe in yourself and your skills

Believing in yourself has certain extraordinary advantages that not only improves your self-confidence but also helps you in achieving your goals.

- It makes you more efficient in terms of your performance and productivity
- Helps you to maintain your focus and sharpen your thought process
- Makes you fight risks and strengthens you to face challenges

Improve yourself belief for a better tomorrow by practicing meditation, yoga, reading, etc.

Self belief fortunes success

Way no. 319 to successful selling

Visit expos to upgrade yourself

Visiting exhibitions, attending seminars etc is highly recommended as it adds to your knowledge about the products / services in market.

It benefits you in understanding 3 important aspects:

- Competitors
- Sales strategies
- Customer requirements

Keep a tab

Way no. 320 to successful selling

Pricing with 9

Everyone knows that $ 100/- and $ 99/- differ marginally. But due to human psychology of saving, we always get attracted towards pricing on products / services ending with $9, $99 $999 . . . . And so on!

Research proves that individuals will not hesitate spending thousands' on shopping, but their bills will always include price tags of $9/-$99/- etc on their products / services.

You need to take this advantage of playing with numbers and displaying them in a manner where it appears a less digit pricing on your products / services.

Pricing tactfully

Way no. 321 to successful selling

Spending habit of a customer

Analyze a particular customer' spending habits by observing his presentation and surroundings. This helps you in qualifying the customer for your product / service.

How to analyze spending habits:

- Overall appearance
- Standard of living
- Social presence
- Profile
- Family

Study well

Way no. 322 to successful selling

Fear of rejection

Do not ever bring fear of rejection in your mind. This will make you lose your confidence and willingness to sell.

Fear of rejection will be noticed in your sales approach, as it will constantly send signals that this customer will not buy.

You need to overcome these thoughts before any calls/ meetings and then move ahead.

Basic reasons for fear of rejection may be :

- Consecutive failures in past
- Lack of product knowledge
- Difficult customer
- Close to target deadlines
- Thinking only about worst consequences

Fight fear

Way no. 323 to successful selling

Learn from every sales call / meeting

A successful sales professionals always studies their call / meeting and try to understand what they did the best that helped them achieve business OR the reasons behind the loss of the deal on any particular call / meeting.

Their experiences with their prospective customers are closely observed by them and such sales professionals learn from their calls / meetings.

Learning

Way no. 324 to successful selling

Some people only assure buying, but never buy

And there are such people also in existence, just to annoy and frustrate sales professionals.

These people will try their level best to convince you that they are genuine buyers and they will demand fair bit of your precious time in explaining your product/service for more than 2-3 times.

They will not even hesitate to waste your marketing material and ask for personal favors like transport facility, office resources etc, which you may entertain in expectation of a sale.

Even after addressing their concerns repeatedly, they will promise and vanish. You may end up falling prey to such customers.

Learn to identify such people on time to save your time for more prospective clients.

Do not fall for over-promising Prospects

Way no. 325 to successful selling

These things will hold you back

Assumptions	Bad attitude	Bad company
Bad mouthing	Cheating	Demoralization
Differences	False promises	Fear
Fraud	Greed	Ignorance
Illness	Insincerity	Laziness
Messiness	Misbehavior	Misguidance
Negativity	Non cooperation	Only talking
Being pushy	Repeated mistakes	Rudeness
Shortcuts	Shyness	Tension
Being timid	Unprepared	Worry

Bad things

Way no. 326 to successful selling

These things will support you

Ambition	Boldness	Confidence
Cooperation	Courage	Dream big
Focus	Good attitude	Good behavior
Good company	Hard work	Good Health
Listening	Mission	Mistakes
Multitasking	Patience	Performance
Persistence	Planning	Politeness
Positivity	Punctuality	Reading
Responsibility	Sincerity	Smile
Teamwork	Trustworthiness	Vision

Good things

Way no. 327 to successful selling

Make others feel important and significant

Make other people feel important, because we all love to feel important, its human psychology.

All like to be praised. By doing so, you are impressing them and gradually starting to disclose your interests. It's a smooth selling process for your products / services.

Praise your customers' achievements and progress. They will be very glad and will often keep in contact with you for all their needs. Such practice shows that you are concerned for your customer and your sales are always on the rise.

All are important

Way no. 328 to successful selling

Utilize everything available

You are surrounded with many useful resources which go unnoticed like research team, production house, your vendors, etc. One has to be smart enough to make the best use of these available resources.

Examples:

- Visiting your vendors' office to explore opportunities will always benefit you with more business.
- If you are new in company, compare old brochures with the new ones, to understand newly added features and benefits.
- Your production house will always feed you with thorough knowledge that will add value to your presentations.

Utilize resources wisely

Way no. 329 to successful selling

You will always find a few unhappy customers

It's funny, but real, that there are a few people in this world who just love to keep complaining every now and then.

These are habitual complainers. They have complains' with everything and everyone.

They will surely find a new complain every time you solve the previous one.

It's advisable and profitable to ignore such customer than to entertain and maintain them. The more you try to provide solutions; you are more prone to invite difficulties and may even incur losses.

Some people never change

Way no. 330 to successful selling

Email promotions

One of the finest ways of sales promotion in today's era is "Emails". We come across lots of emails a day and practically acknowledge a few which have a strong subject line.

You also need to consider a strong subject line while sending a promotional email to your customer as this punch line should tempt the reader to open your email instantly. Subject line should be short and self explanatory.

Examples:

- Flat 50% discount only for you
- Weekend loot
- End of season sales
- Exclusively for your employees
- Zero making charges on ornaments

Subject line attracts

Way no. 331 to successful selling

Keep good relations with influential people

Influential people like politicians, industrialists & corporate, social workers etc. prove to be very useful for growth in sales because their recommendations are taken seriously.

Hence maintaining a healthy relation with such people is very important.

Such people will give you business in bulk and will always add valuable network in your contact list.

Influential people = increased sales

Way no. 332 to successful selling

Attend complaints yourself (If any)

It's a known fact that we make the deal but wish to send some other person to attend the complaint. Bad practice. Isn't it?

If you have sold the product, isn't it your duty to attend the complaints?

Do attend the complaints yourself, because you are in a better position to understand your customer. You know exactly, what you promised, and should be delivering the same. This will avoid your customers frustration, if you send someone else, he has to take trouble to make the 3rd person understand the issue. You risk your rapport in the long run, if you neglect complaints, resulting in unsatisfied customers.

You sold, you entertain

Way no. 333 to successful selling

You do not sell, you help in buying

Always meet customers with the intention of helping them to choose the right product / service. You have to first give undivided attention to their requirements, so that they share their needs to you as a family member and expect a genuine solution from you.

A customer will never appreciate if he notices that you are neglecting their concerns and only intend to make profit selfishly.

Do not do selfish sales

Way no. 334 to successful selling

Voice mail box

Remember, no one will call you back until you show them some benefits.

While leaving a voice mail, do remember to record some benefits for them. If a customer finds it interesting, then only he / she will call you back.

You need to start with your name, companies name and purpose of calling in short. At the end repeat your name and number with a good bye note.

Record short and clear message as the receiver may have to check many more voice mails.

Always record some good reason for a call back.

Create call back curiosity

Way no. 335 to successful selling

Study your previous customers closing timeline

Study and research how long did your previous customers take to close the sale.

Make a chart / graph which includes everything between the first call and payment received for every previous customer.

You will notice that many times you took more than usual time with some customers. Study such cases closely.

This will give you a clear idea on how you can shorten the timeline for sales next time.

Closing timeline

Way no. 336 to successful selling

Speaker phone

Ask for permission before placing anyone on speaker phone. If someone wishes to be a part of conversation please do introduce him/her.

People hate to be heard on speaker and find it rude as they are not sure who all are hearing them. It gives the other person a feeling that you are making him heard as an evidence for something personal and is considered as breach of privacy.

It is also noticed that people do not speak freely if they realize that you are talking to them on speaker phone.

Note: If you are dealing with delicate issues, please avoid discussing the same on speaker phone.

Phone etiquette

Way no. 337 to successful selling

Keep asking questions until you get answers

Always ask questions to yourself, your seniors, your employees, clients, etc until you get the satisfactory solution.

Questions starting with the words—how, why, where, what will create curiosity of learning something new in your line of business. Questioning help us to avoid mistakes and result in profitable outcome.

Practicing such techniques of questioning results in becoming more knowledgeable and confident on providing solutions.

When in doubt ask questions

Way no. 338 to successful selling

Allocate time wisely between customers

Customers vary in every manner as they belong to varied professions, cultures, etc.

You may come across individuals who often buy product /service in bulk, but they definitely consume majority of your time to get convinced. Such customer category should be entertained at leisure (Evenings, weekends etc) because they like spending time while buying product / service.

Customers who are always in hurry and hate to waste time should always be considered in mornings as they do not waste your time too and close sale within a few minutes.

Allocate the most productive time (morning) to important customer (big personality customers).

Manage time wisely

Way no. 339 to successful selling

Do not start selling as soon as you meet

Just do not start with your sales pitch as soon as you meet the prospect. It really shows your selfishness.

Instead spend a few minutes in general chats, which will give time to you as well as the opposite person to know each other well. This will build good comfort to start your sales talk.

By doing this you are making a rapport that you have just not come to do sales, but also you keep interest in knowing and caring for the customer.

Take time to settle down

Way no. 340 to successful selling

Fake it till you make it

It's quite true that sometimes you really do not like the product / service you are selling, and even do not believe in it.

But due to some personal circumstances you need to keep going. If this is your case, then do your best to fake the feeling of liking what you are doing. It is really difficult to do so, but you have to do it.

Remember the reason you made the decision and opted to sell the product / service. Encourage yourself to find good things in your product / service that benefit you (monetary and recognition), and the moment you come across the key benefits, it automatically drives you to make sales.

Imitate for betterment

Way no. 341 to successful selling

Give non-precious gifts

Giving away gifts to clients is an old idea of keeping in steady relations.

But do not ever give expensive gifts, as they account for bribe.

Gifts are given as a good gesture and for thanks giving motive.

Gift should be chosen wisely. It should be something that will be in front of your customers or of daily use, so that every day they see / use it and remember you.

Examples: stationeries, accessories, etc.

Gifts

Way no. 342 to successful selling

Do not depend on email and text messages

It is advisable that you should not wait for someone to reply when you have emailed / texted them.

If you think that you have spent enough time waiting for the other person's reply, do not hesitate to approach them in person or ensure you make a call to get the exact status about the situation that's being discussed.

There may be several reasons for not responding, like:

- He must have forgotten, due to his work load
- May be on tour
- No access to network
- Due to some unexpected incident

Upfront approach

Way no. 343 to successful selling

Your personality will help you for first few minutes

Your charming personality will help you for first few minutes, after that, your product knowledge, skills and presentation will.

Your personality is just a gate pass to get introduced to your customer. A good personality is important to get attention from customers, **that's it**. It is just a means of getting welcomed.

It should not be mistaken that your pleasing personality will get you sales.

Limited advantage

Way no. 344 to successful selling

Prequalified products

If you have products / services of high range where your customer needs financial help to buy them, ensure you visit them with a financial advisor prepared with required formalities.

Products like Property, Vehicles etc always have prequalified loan facilities for customers benefit.

Example:
If you are visiting a customer who is prepared to buy a car or house, ask your banker to accompany you with all documents for loan formalities. This will make your customer more certain on his decision of buying the product / service. It also helps your customer to understand and plan his finances accordingly.

When you practice these methods of being prepared for the prequalified products, you are always looked upon as a thorough professional.

Prequalified limits = Advantage

Way no. 345 to successful selling

Do not say "you cannot buy this"

Many times you will come across with people who need your product/service, but really can't afford.

In such cases, do not ever say that "you cannot buy this or afford this, as this is costly for you".

Instead, work out some discount, EMI, or atleast suggest some other lower range product, with less features than yours.

But, never let them feel that they cannot buy your product/service just because they are short of funds.

Be helpful

Way no. 346 to successful selling

Recession

One must consider the economic fact "Recession".

During such periods you should start making relations with as many people as you can. Visit maximum customers at their door step, tell about your product/ service without asking them to buy.

This will save a lot of time when economic crisis disappear because you will have customers who already know about your product/service.

However recession in real estate and other investment businesses can be of benefit as customers may get a good bargain for the product /service and will also get good returns once recession is over.

Increase your network

Way no. 347 to successful selling

Locked up situation

This is a great situation; people sitting next to you are bound to listen, even if they do not wish to.

When you are traveling long distance (by air or inter-state train / bus), you know how much time it's going to take for the journey, and the people around you will be eager to talk to you for passing time.

Take full advantages of this situation to tell them about your business. Off course, you should start with general chat first, and tactfully initiate your solicitation of business.

Captive prospects

Way no. 348 to successful selling

Price doesn't matter, but your selling skill does

We have heard this sentence many times from sales people—'I could have managed more sales if price of the product were lower'.

In actual, it's not true at all.
If you think your price is too high, you will unknowingly pass this message to customers also.
Instead, justify yourself that the cost is reasonable and your product / service deserves it.

Aren't people buying expensive watches? The time these watches display is the same as displayed on non-expensive watches.

When you can convince wisely and justify your product / service, price tag does not really matter for closing sales.

Be proud of your price

Way no. 349 to successful selling

Improve your performance sale after sale

Look for improvements in your performance day after day.

If your target for this week is 10 sales then it should be 12 in next week and so on. Slowly increase your targets, for that you need to sale more wisely, find some more techniques, some more strategies, and more time too.

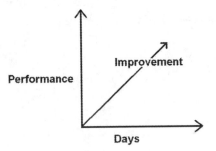

Perform better every time to achieve more every time.

Keep improving

Way no. 350 to successful selling

Go for training atleast once a year

You need to attend a sales training / course / seminar atleast once a year.

If you are working for some company, then it's for your own benefit as well as for your employer. There may be situations that xyz employers do not have any such training sessions or you may be a independent sales businessman, In such cases, join at your own cost as it is for yourself development.

Such training sessions help you boost your thinking and make you learn new approaches required for sales. Professional training is one of the best methods that help you to keep pace with today's world.

Train yourself

Way no. 351 to successful selling

Entertain clients for reasonable time

Learn to entertain each client for a reasonable time. Do not make too short nor too long. If you think the client is wasting too much of time without showing any interest of buying, then it's time to take his permission and leave. Do follow up such clients on phone next time. Only attend them next time if they show some interest in buying.

Practically, you get to know the buying intentions of a customer in 2-3 meetings, and if they do not show interest even after 6 follow ups. Do not call them; they are not going to buy from you.

Reasonable time

Way no. 352 to successful selling

Giving too much information is unhealthy

Giving too much information will confuse the customer.

Give exactly the amount of information required to conclude the sale otherwise you are just wasting your as well as their time. If you just bombard them with your sales talk, they will just walk out.

A customer who wants to buy a car requires information on comfort, mileage, cost that's it. If you give him info on capacity of engine, the thickness of chassis, some technology used in fuel intake system, etc . . . He will get puzzled and just delay the decision of buying.

Give appropriate information

Way no. 353 to successful selling

Do not talk too much

Though its necessary to give time to customer to close the deal. But time allocated should be reasonable.

If you are not sure that the customer is going to buy from you now, then there is no reason to extend the meeting. You should wisely get your time utilized for the most productive deal and carry on with your further appointments.

Remember the more people you meet the more business you get.

Time is money

Way no. 354 to successful selling

Delegate your non-essential work to someone

Many of us have a habit of doing all the work ourselves to ensure perfectness. But all the work includes many non-selling and distracting activities too.

Give non-selling work like—filing, putting data into computers, arranging business cards, giving broachers for printing, collecting dues, arrangements of seminars, booking tickets for business trips, fixing appointments for dentist, etc to your secretary as you risk focus.

This way you get time to focus on your actual business, i.e., "Sales".

Work smarter, not harder

Way no. 355 to successful selling

Higher price tag next to your product display

One of the tricks that you will definitely succeed in, is tagging your product/ service next to a similar one which is costlier than yours.

When you approach customers with similar products/ services with two different price tags they tend to opt for the product/ service with a lesser price.

Example:

You approach a customer with 2 pens with identical features, benefits & warranty but different cost on it.
Your customer will buy the pen with lesser price tag & you will accordingly achieve your desired target.

Present wisely

Way no. 356 to successful selling

Reach 5-10 minutes before time

As old saying goes—"respect time and time will respect you".

The opposite person has found time out of his busy schedule for you and you need to value it.
Accordingly, time is equally important for you too, as it shall give you an opening for your business.

If you reach late for any appointment, the chances are you may be asked to wait, or asked to leave and take appointment on some other day or even worst that you may not get the appointment in near future.

Respect time, yours as well as other persons.

Respect time

Way no. 357 to successful selling

Take your colleague with you when meeting big customers

Always ask your colleague to accompany you when you have meeting with a big customer.

Big customers throw many questions / objections. You alone may fall short to answer all their queries. In such situations your colleague will take over the conversation.

And it's a good impression on the customer too, as he thinks you are not alone and you have come prepared with your team.

More the merrier

Way no. 358 to successful selling

Be plural

You have to be vast in your approach in sales business. While giving example do not be specific to a particular individual, rather be plural and address saying that "many of our customers have benefited from your product / services". By doing so you put whole group of people in front of your customer for comparison.

Practice this technique as it portrays that you have a upper hand in your past sales experience amongst the whole group of people.

Use sentences like:

- We have so many customers enjoying our products / services.
- Several of our customers have benefited from our products / services.

Majority attracts

Way no. 359 to successful selling

Wear dark suits for meetings

Wear dark suits (preferably black or dark blue) for meetings.

Dark colors are commanding & reflect authority, smartness and ready to take the world in your attitude.

Be smart to show your presence.

Ever noticed, when you suddenly see someone in black suit, what impression it leaves on your mind?
You find that person more powerful than others.

Dark colors appeal

Way no. 360 to successful selling

Always be optimistic

There is nothing called 'bad luck' as such. The only luck, I ever came across is a good luck.

Pessimists take help of such words to cover their failures . . .
Success is not merely a matter of luck. Good luck doesn't happen by chance, you have to work at it.

Situations seem difficult because we do not dare to solve them. If you try to solve them, you will see opportunities in every difficulty.

Note: If you are pessimist you will see difficulty in every opportunity.

Only "Good luck"

Way no. 361 to successful selling

Do not argue with your customer

Do not ever get into argument/difference of opinion with your customer.

Such situations may arise when you are in discussion with your customer on issues that gave them a negative experience / if the customer is disturbed.

To get best deal from customers, avoid arguments. Argument will leave a bad report & you will lose the sale.

You will win the battle, but lose the sale.

Avoid arguments

Way no. 362 to successful selling

Understand difference between Hearing and Listening

Though hearing and listening seems very much similar, but actually these two are very different.

- Hearing is a physical act.

- Listening is a mental act.

Hearing is merely one of the 5 senses that relates only physical aspect and not necessarily need a response from the brain.

Whereas listening is a process, step ahead from hearing, as it takes your brain to respond to everything it hears'. Listening is a method used in communication to make the opposite person aware that you are acknowledging to everything uttered by them.

Listen actively

Way no. 363 to successful selling

Come out of your comfort zone

Comfort zone refers to an individual's behavioral state in which he operates at ease. In this state operations are risk-free and deliver steady level of performance.

In order to extract optimum results from your performances you need to come out of this comfort zone, and precisely experiment new horizon.

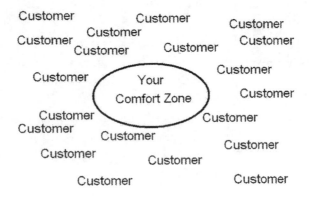

Leave comfort zone

Way no. 364 to successful selling

Narrate stories

One of the valuable sales strategies that proves effective in making sales is narrating stories of your old / existing customers and their experiences.

You majorly come across some common objections from your customers for not buying your product / service. In such situations recollect your past experience when you were able to handle the objection with solution and made your sales, narrate the same story to your current customer and you come more close to make a sale again.

Your story always helps the customer get connected to your past customer who had similar objection for your product / service and when you share the solution, your new customer agrees to buy from you.

Stories connect

Way no. 365 to successful selling

Keep customers hooked up

Unless you hear a perfect "NO" from anyone keep your product/service alive in his mind.

Do not call customers more than 5-6 times.

Learn to keep their interest alive in your product, because many people see and check the product but forget due to their busy schedules.

Just keep sending them short updates on emails or through text messages. May be after a while they may ask you for a few details and close the deal.

Do not stop until you hear "NO"

Way no. 366 to successful selling

Customer service

Closing the deal is not the end of the sales business; it's the start of new relationship. One needs to learn to keep customers satisfied at all the times.

Attending complain with the following aspects in mind will help:

- Listen to complains politely
- Be accessible for customer
- Do not argue
- If you had over promised and under delivered, accept it and please correct it.
- Be caring as a problem solver
- Respect the customer.
- Just do what you said you will do.
- Don't lose your customer.

Note: A single unhappy customer will shares his experiences with as many as 10 people. But a happy customer will share it with only 3-4 people.

At your service sir / mam!

Way no. 367 to successful selling

Some common buying signals

These are some common buying signals which prospects gives us while still in discussion:

- Discounts
- Payment mode
- Colors available
- After sales service
- Guarantee/warrantee
- Enquiry on delivery date
- Any freebees with product
- Option of monthly installments
- Asks only product related questions
- Reads broucher/manual with high interest

Understand hints

Way no. 368 to successful selling

Do what you are afraid of doing

Every sales professional goes through this phase during his initial days in sales industry, as the person is new and unaware with the experience of attending customers.

It is their fear of trying something new that they have never tried, but gradually overcome it. You need to remember these instances as it will help you face up the challenges instead of being frightened.

You may come across difficult customers, situations etc. Do not get afraid of failure; instead make an effort to face it. This will always strengthen you to take challenges and your fear will cease to exist.

Fear disappears

Way no. 369 to successful selling

Blame yourself for failure

People blame the whole world for their failure, but is it true? No way. Just think aren't we the actual problem, if we fail to do something?

It is you, who is responsible for the failure.

Who got affected by failure? Whole world or you alone? So, if you fail, it's your problem.

Try to solve it rather than blaming others and the circumstances for failures.

Blame yourself and next time sales is guaranteed.

You failed

Way no. 370 to successful selling

When new business, protect the downside

Whenever you are, new in business or if there is a launch of new product, please do protect the downside, because new things may not necessarily work as planned. It might take time than you predicted, or the market conditions may change unexpectedly.

Always have a survival plan for a long run in such situations. Do not completely leave your old product/ business/ job when trying something new.

Plan in such a way that if the new concept fails, you still have a back up and revenue from your old product / service.

Play safe

Way no. 371 to successful selling

Take your colleague with you

If possible, take a colleague with you for a meeting. Not to train him / her on sales, but to take notes on your sales approach.

Let him closely observe and monitor the complete discussion between you and the other members present.

After the meeting, ask him for feedback on your performance.

Take feedback from him, and try to improve in areas where he found some improvement is needed.

Go in pair

Way no. 372 to successful selling

Get along with everyone

People who get along with everyone make a good salesperson.

You need to get trained yourself to get friendly and emotionally connected to every type of person in society.

Many people will not allow you to get into their comfort zone easily. You need to find out some way around to get into their circle through their other friends or any other social place where they are available and you can get their attention.

A good sales person should have a welcoming and friendly attitude which helps him to makes friends quickly.

Get glued to all

Way no. 373 to successful selling

Be serious with sales, all the time

We take things seriously only when we find ourselves in trouble, or slightly before the trouble starts.

If, we are on toes all the time, then such situations do not arise.

Assume, the trouble is just around the corner and you need to work hard to keep it away.

Following the deadlines by achieving your daily/weekly goals keeps you racing ahead of bad times.

Seriousness counts

Way no. 374 to successful selling

Keep a log of people who did not buy from you

Do keep a log of people who did not buy from you.

Keep their contact details, reasons for not buying. And write your remark for not concluding the sale.

This is very important way to learn, what went wrong. There are chances that it may be a wrong approach which did not match to the other person's attitude.

Find out ways to tackle such people in future.

And you could approach the same people from this log after some time for a second trial of sales.

Learning's from non-buyers

Way no. 375 to successful selling

Qualities of an unsuccessful salesperson

These are a few qualities you will find in a unsuccessful salesperson:

- Rarely smiles
- Not so confident
- Not willing to be helpful
- They themselves have many problems
- They demoralize others
- Least enthusiastic
- Lack luster attitude
- Do not follow up customers
- Just want to make fast bucks

Need to practice

Way no. 376 to successful selling

Understand buying motive of customers

There has to be a buying motive behind every purchase. Smart sales professionals try to find out the reasons behind buying their products / services.

If the motive is known, sale becomes easy.

Like in case of properties . . . if you know the buyer is an end-user or an investor, you can suggest him properties accordingly.

Another example . . . if a person wants to buy books, he wants them for himself or wants to setup a library for poor people . . . you can set discount/offer accordingly.

Understand buying motive

Way no. 377 to successful selling

Stick to your commitments

Be committed in everything you do.

It may be a promise you made to some client or it may be a deadline of your targets.

Once the customer has experienced your commitment in work, he will always prefer to buy only from you and will surely want his loved ones to enjoy your product/services. You will always be recommended in the long run.

Being committed to your deadlines / targets will make you punctual and consistent in delivering good results.

Be committed

Way no. 378 to successful selling

Avoid people who doubt your goals / targets

Its recommended that you distance yourself from people who say "you cannot do it".

These people are those who themselves have not achieved anything noticeable in their own life.

These are non performers and non achievers, and they just love to pull people backward/ down, and want them to fail too.

Listening to these people is really dangerous. Their words will pull down your confidence, and feed negative concerns in your mind.

Avoid losers

Way no. 379 to successful selling

A thing becomes necessity, when your neighbour has it

Sales professionals usually fail to notice easiest opportunity available next door to your existing customer.

It is a common phenomenon observed with every person 'I want xyz product/services because my neighbors have it'. This egoistic feeling becomes a opportunity for you and a very simple deal to win.

Just to prove their superiority they rarely bargain & tend to buy exclusive goods in higher quantities.

Others ego = your business

Way no. 380 to successful selling

Create a structure for loyal customers

Create a structure for your loyal customers, who repeat business with you.

It can be a reward programme like giving 5-10% discounts if they purchase within 6 months or 1 year, some points on their every purchase, which can be redeemed for some gifts or further discounts, etc. for some specific period.

Organize some lucky draw, and actually give something to the winner, and include their story or picture in your newsletters or broachers, etc., can be witness by other customers.

All this will encourage them to buy more from you.

Loyalty pays

Way no. 381 to successful selling

Middle price sales

People hesitate to buy products of higher and lower range, and opt to buy the middle range product/service due to 2 basic reasons:

They do not want to buy the cheapest available.
They do not want to spend on the highest, when a middle range is available.

This is a human tendency. and can be used tactfully during the launch of your new product/service.

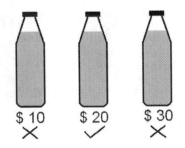

Human tendencies

Way no. 382 to successful selling

Type of questions customer ask

Generally, customers ask us 2 type of questions while presentation. One is "Testing" question and the other one is "update me" question.

Testing question:
Such questions are asked to test your knowledge, skill, talent, etc. These are your qualifying round questions. If the customer is satisfied with your answers, then only further discussion is possible.

Update me questions:
These questions are the actual information gathering questions. Customer shows interest in your product / service and wants to know more about it. These questions are part of sales progress.

Answer them all

Way no. 383 to successful selling

When you get a 'YES', take order immidietly

When the prospect has agreed buying your product/service, just stop your sales pitch and take out the order form. Do not waste your time in explaining more of your product/service.

The buyer must be aware of your product/service, and you have explained whatever he wanted to know more about it.

At such moments, respect his talent and decision making power and just close the deal.

Your extra unwanted information may spoil the deal.

Strike the deal

Way no. 384 to successful selling

Know your competitor

You need to gather the following information of your competitor for your betterment:

- Are they making profits?
- How long in business?
- Size of their company.
- Their achievements
- Their customer reviews.
- Their expansion plans.
- Their growth rate.
- Their market share in percentage.
- Their operating areas.
- Their pricing structure.
- Their range of products.
- Their strategies for sales and marketing.
- Volume of their business.
- What are their revenues?

Be updated

Way no. 385 to successful selling

Be a 'how' thinker and not 'if' thinker

HOW thinking:
It leads to a powerful activation of your brain cells to get associated with solutions on improving the current situation. It helps you to explore new ideas to come up with conclusions for any complex difficulties. How thinking opens possible opportunities/ solutions.

IF thinking:
It leads an individual to limit his/her thought process as it gives you close ended answers on any particular issue. Hence it is recommended to avoid IF thinking. If thinkers always cushion their inabilities with excuses.

Think "HOW"

Way no. 386 to successful selling

Emotion + Logic = Deal

You need to get connected with your customer with the right amount of emotion and then giving logical reasons to buy.

It is the emotion of an individual that triggers buying signals and later the customers applies logic to make the decision of buying.

Example:

A Childs' emotion of happiness makes his father decide logically to buy an affordable toy for him.

The above example narrates a clear understanding why a particular customer tends to take emotional buying decision and later applies logical reasoning according to his comfort.

Emotion sales

Way no. 387 to successful selling

Complete all tasks

Many times you excitedly undertake multiple tasks randomly with intentions of completing, but are unable to complete them.

You need to avoid such practice as it will lead you to repeated failures.

In order improve productivity & maintain a consistent performance you need to complete task's in a systematic manner.

Leaving many tasks incomplete will make you *master of all, but good for nothing.*

One at a time

Way no. 388 to successful selling

Study competitors' weaknesses and strengths

In order to maintain your position in sales industry, you have to be well-informed with your competitors' strengths and weaknesses.

The future of your products / services is depended on sales, and to maintain incremental order supply you also need to be aware of your competitors' sales strategies, promotion methods, details of his product / service, their loop holes and weaknesses etc.

Once you are conscious of their strengths and weaknesses you are in a better position to play your cards for your product / service.

Be alert

Way no. 389 to successful selling

Appoint informal helpers/associates

Make verbal contracts with people like household helpers, painters, watchmen, laundry persons, waiters, barbers, delivery boys, general stores, etc . . .

Basically the idea behind getting associated with these people is, since they are on a constant move and they are more prone to spot requirement of your products / services. In exchange for every sale, you can always share a small commission with them.

It really works.

Take help from everyone possible

Way no. 390 to successful selling

Share bad news too

If anything unexpected happens like delay in delivery, change in price, some changes in specifications of your product / service at the time of delivery or making sales, please share it with customer as soon as possible.

Hiding the fact and then disclosing later is definitely going to annoy your customer and reveal unprofessionalism.

On the other hand, if you share the bad news with customers, the trust bond grows stronger. If possible, try to compensate the inconvenience with an added advantage for your customer. They will always cherish your efforts and lead to customer satisfaction.

Maintain transparency

Way no. 391 to successful selling

Customer is NOT always right

A customer is always right is an old misconception which does not relate in todays era.

At times customers do pretend to be serious buyers & keep you occupied or even after buying they make misleading claims which seem to be valid.

These types of customers may come up with reasons like:

- Replacements
- Refunds
- Dissatisfaction
- False claims
- Unethical claims (self-damaging the product)
- Wrongly chosen product/service by customer

Be aware

Way no. 392 to successful selling

Work for more than 8 hours a day

Many countries follow 5 days a week working schedule. This amounts to only 40 hours working in a week.

This is what average people work for.

Cut down your watching TV or meeting friends in evening or weekends. All these things are not productive, these are pass times.

Start working on Saturday, and add 1 hour daily in every working day. This comes to 54 hours.

Now you have got 35% more working hours which is 35% jump in your sales straight away.

Successful sales professionals work averagely 60-70 hours a week. That's why they are successful.

Work more = get more

Way no. 393 to successful selling

Follow deadlines

Deadline is a key to make sure that sales professionals/ organization are prospering. Deadlines are commitments that keep you focused for achieving timely goals.

Meeting deadlines favors you in several ways, like:

- Adds to credibility
- Boosts productivity
- Enhances relationships
- Improves skills
- Preciseness
- Timely profits
- Seriousness
- Efficiency
- Motivation

Deadlines impact

Way no. 394 to successful selling

Sales doesn't happen by chance, it needs to be planned

Sales is a broader concept and is a result of deep study involving every step starting from your product / services to the end user.

Following points need to be considered while planning:

- Product / service knowledge
- Features and benefits
- Sales and marketing strategies
- Analyzing prospects
- Customer qualification
- Sales presentation
- Trial closures
- Clarifying objections
- Explaining terms and conditions
- Closings
- Feedback and references

Planning is a must

Way no. 395 to successful selling

Be active while presenting

Active sales person always delights people around and is always welcomed. Your activeness proves when you use hand gestures, eye contact, voice modulation, etc.

Being active benefits in following ways:

- Holds customers interest
- Shows confidence
- Impacts positively
- Keeps you focused
- Good results
- Clarity & correctness
- Avoids errors
- Stimulates thought process

Active you, active all

Way no. 396 to successful selling

Promise less, deliver more

It is commonly observed that customers do not expect anything extra once the deal is done. A very general perception they follow is, "what they saw, is what they will get".

You need to mend this universal belief and make an effort to offer something extra than your standard product / service.

Example:
You may want to add a big soft toy with the delivery of new car, as customer has come with his kids to take the keys. This will definitely delight them.

People appreciate and love this way of delivering.

People love good surprises

Way no. 397 to successful selling

Get yourself known as a result-oriented sales person

In today's competitive world, your mere existence as a sales person is just not enough, as you will be just one amongst the crowd.

Consistence in your performance will reward you in becoming a result-oriented sales person.

Benefits of being a result-oriented sales person:

- Good appreciation
- Satisfied customers
- High profits
- Pride and recognition
- Customer confidence
- Improves productivity

Be result-oriented

Way no. 398 to successful selling

Always ask yourself these questions . . .

Always ask these to yourself for better growth of business:

- Are you utilizing your full potential?
- Is your current network sufficient to achieve targets?
- What are your average sales?
- Can you beat the competition?
- How can you improve your performance?
- How many channels do you have for promotions?
- Is your current sales team strength, sufficient and well trained?
- Do you have required infrastructure or sales material needed to make sales promotion?
- Are you working on genuine feed backs from existing?

Self help

Way no. 399 to successful selling

Do not address customers by their first name

Do not address people by their first name unless they are younger than you or too friendly with you.

Unless and until permitted by the customer do not address them by their first name.

Addressing customers by their first names impacts negatively in following manners:

- Sounds rude
- Arrogant attitude
- They feel offended
- They feel less valued
- Sounds unprofessional
- Can lead to dispute

Address respectfully

Way no. 400 to successful selling

Create a network of networks

Networking is the best way to multiply your sales in a big way.

Make a network of networks. It means identifying customers within your network who have their own network of customers. Entering such group will certainly save your time and money.

When you maintain your presence amongst your customers' network, it becomes easy for you to make sales.

Since you have already made an influential customer and the same customer is helping you establish your product / service within his network.

Do networking

Way no. 401 to successful selling

Email or text message after call / meeting

It's a good practice to send an email or a text message immediately after calling/meeting any customer. It gives a feeling that you value them.

Why this is necessary:

- To show gratitude
- Sincerity
- Personal touch
- Rapport
- Branding and advertising
- Simple and convenient
- Confirmation on black and white

Reciprocate

Way no. 402 to successful selling

Change your presentation according to customers

Same strategies and skills cannot be used on all the customers you meet. You need to adjust according to the customers comfort, need, demands, etc.

Avoid giving presentation like a learnt parrot, who no matter whom he sees, talks the same thing to everyone.

Example:

If you are selling a wrist watch to a rich and wealthy personality, you cannot approach him with a variety of regular wrist watches, instead you need to understand his requirement of high end brands and present accordingly.

Different people, different approaches

Way no. 403 to successful selling

Be ambitious in whatever you do

Ambition to achieve a specific target is very important, without which nothing really moves in this world. All great achievers have a strong ambition to achieve their goals.

Advantages of being ambitious:

- Dignity and greatness
- Disciplined achievement
- Bright future
- Enhances creativity
- Constructive approach
- Sharpens skills
- Leadership

Be ambitious

Way no. 404 to successful selling

Give only the information which is necessary for a sale

It is really useless to waste time in giving all the information at one go. This creates confusion for your customer. You need to share only useful information that is necessary during a sale.

Example:

While selling a mobile phone to an old customer, you would definitely like to give the best of facilities and features like android service, xyz messengers', etc, this will always confuse them and he may ignore to buy from you. Instead ask for his basic requirements and accordingly approach with a specific model more suitable for them.

Avoid giving unwanted info

Way no. 405 to successful selling

Gut feeling

Gut feeling is a blend of positive or negative feelings combined with emotional intuitions.

In sales, it's the mechanism which drives your sub-conscious mind, and takes your actual mind towards a sale.

A positive gut feeling comes from:

- Your skills
- Confidence and knowledge.
- You have a prospective database.
- Favorable conditions.
- Experience
- Good response for your product/service

X-factor

Way no. 406 to successful selling

Find strong reasons why customer should buy from you

Find out most strong reasons, why a customer should buy your product/service from you and not from your competitors.

It will prepare you in advance to handle objections and clarify them on the spot. Make this list in written form and practice the same with your team during meetings.

These reasons should be convincing enough with guaranteeing sure shot buying points for a customer.

Examples:

- Most fuel efficient car till date
- HD picture quality for every channel
- Long lasting battery life in mobile phones
- Guaranteed returns on savings and investments

Make sale with strong reasons

Way no. 407 to successful selling

Features Vs Benefits

<u>Feature</u>:

It is an unique characteristic of the product/service that sets it apart from similar items. These are measurable and are an important aspect of every product/service.

<u>Benefit</u>:

It's the solution/gain from a feature of a particular product/service which a customer enjoys. A benefit fulfils the customers need. It is the actual factor (performance, design etc) that satisfies customers' needs & wants.

Customers buy benefits

Way no. 408 to successful selling

When customer abandon online purchase

These are some reasons customer may abandon during purchasing from an online site:

- Complicated registration process
- Problem signing in
- Too many newsletters and promos bombarded
- Doubt website security
- Website difficult to navigate
- Lack of information on product/service
- No one answered/replied their query
- Help line not really helpful
- Check out problems
- Delivery cost too high and unrealistic
- Product / services out of stock
- Want to reconsider his buying

Online selling

Way no. 409 to successful selling

If you are not consistent, then you are moving backwards

Keep moving ahead consistently. Because if you are not consistent then it means you are moving backward, falling behind and eventually you are going to fail some day.

Why being consistent matters:

- Better performance
- No failure
- Achievement of targets and goals
- Strong bonding with customers
- Appreciation by people
- Organized
- Enhances creativity
- Rewarding results
- Excelling profile

Be consistent

Way no. 410 to successful selling

See new customer as soon as possible

Whenever you get a call from a new customer showing interest in your product/service, or some good friend/ customer of yours has suggested a new possible buyer to you, do not delay in calling and meeting him.

You should make sure you meet them as soon as possible, because the excitement and enthusiasm is at the highest peak when you hear about new customer. It may not be same and will start getting lower as time goes.

You won't sound that energetic and exited if you meet him after weeks/months and this will affect your sales presentation. Later they will be just a hit-or-miss type of customer.

Run to new customers ASAP

Way no. 411 to successful selling

Who is prospect?

Prospect is someone who has a specific need and could buy from you.

A person can be counted as a prospect when:

- He/she who has the buying authority.
- He/she qualifies for your product/services
- He/she thinks you can help him/her buy
- He/she inquire about product/service
- He/she agrees to see product/service
- He/she calls you again for clarifications
- He/she raises objections
- He/she shows curiosity/interest in your product/ service

Good prospect = future customer

Way no. 412 to successful selling

Can you help me out?

We all love to help each other. This is human psychology. Why not make use of this in-built feature of ours?

If you start with traditional sentence, like—Hello!, I am Mr. Abc from Xyz Company, and I am here to give demo of new product . . . . etc., you will get a traditional response which we all hate, i.e. "NO".

But think what happens if you approach in other fashion, like—

What if you start with this sentence—"Excuse me, can you help me out?"

Here you have broken the ice. When you ask for help, you get it. Customer will see how he/she can be of any help in closing a deal.

Note: Ideal for telemarketing and door-to-door salesperson.

Excuse me . . .

Way no. 413 to successful selling

Thanking for everything

Sales is about establishing and maintaining excellent relationship, a thanking note always adds value to enhance a bonding.

A 'thank you' shows that we value the customer and respect them. It also denotes that we are grateful for the opportunity in associating with them.

A thank you can be addressed in several ways :

- Verbal / written thank you
- Flowers and chocolates
- Gift hampers/vouchers/coupons
- Non precious gifts

Thank them for the business

Way no. 414 to successful selling

People who buy only by price are not loyal customers

People who are price centered, and do not care much about the long term benefits of your product/service, will not give you much margin and are not among the loyal ones.

Such customers tend to switch suppliers very often.
Even these people bad mouth your product to save some extra money to buy similar product from your competitor.

You have to be careful enough to understand such buyers as you may make sales to such customers but you will risk your credibility in future.

Sell wisely

Way no. 415 to successful selling

Being different than others will help

Being different for right reasons is wise idea.

Show that you are different than other sales persons and your product/service is also very different than others.

Customers always get influenced when you present yourself different than others, by using different approaches, techniques, ideas, presentations, etc.

Being different will always get you a special recognition and add value to your efforts. Your achievements will also be extraordinary.

Being different, results different

Way no. 416 to successful selling

A close is not the end of sales

A close is not the end of a sale, it's just half of the business because after sales you need to keep the customer satisfied by maintaining trust and asking for referrals.

See every satisfied customer as 1+ ... customer as their recommendations will get more customers in future.

Example:

A professional from real estate industry always advantages good business from existing customers as they refer his name to their guests and visitors.

The above example proves that even if you close the sale it does not mean an end.

Keep the balls rolling

Way no. 417 to successful selling

Maintain good health

Maintaining good health is vital for every sales person. A healthy person seems delighted & is always welcomed by all.

Good health will ensure that you do not cancel any appointments as no customer likes to postpone or cancel meetings. Eventually, your chances of getting next appointment are 50:50 or nil.

Advantages of being healthy:

- Good performance
- Punctuality
- Customer satisfaction
- Efficient working
- Appreciation
- More business

Stay fit, stay healthy

Way no. 418 to successful selling

When to start negotiation

Many sales professionals do not know, 'when and who' starts negotiation. Customer has to agree buying from you and that is when your customer initiates negotiation. It is a process after you have finished your sales presentation.

Negotiation is getting in agreement of closing the order, which is beneficial to both parties, and only limited points can be considered for negotiation:

- Payment schedule
- Time of delivery
- Terms and conditions
- Product / service
- Special benefits
- Additional business / bulk orders

Negotiation leads to sales

Way no. 419 to successful selling

Stay busy

At times you may think that the days' work is done early, and think of passing time watching TV or packing up. But utilizing those minutes/hours in staying busy will bring business in future.

Staying busy means doing some productive work, like finding new strategies, getting information about competitor, calling some old customer, etc.

Staying busy gives a psychological boost to our mind. The more you keep yourself occupied, the more work gets done, and that too very smoothly without much extra efforts.

Stay busy, stay loaded

Way no. 420 to successful selling

Be polite . . . . be calm

Always be polite on calls as well as in meetings. Being polite is best way to make new relationships.

Whenever you come across a difficult customer, or a person who is wasting your time for nothing, be polite and instead of listening to him, just get up politely and move on to other call/meeting.

Use sentences like:

- Please may I take your leave
- May be we can discuss this later
- Pleasure meeting you
- I will be glad to see you again
- Can I be of any more help to you?

Be polite /calm

Way no. 421 to successful selling

When in tension, worry, problems, etc . . . . sales will not happen

Your state of mind majorly affects on your sales performance. When you are tensed or worried, it portrays in your approach, and you become prone to commit mistakes while performing.

Hazards of continuing in such stages:

- Losing face due to bad presentation
- Losing a customer/business
- Misleading information
- Over commitment
- Revealing your personal issues
- Misusing company recourses
- Affects your routine

Tension, worry, problem . . . loss of business

Way no. 422 to successful selling

Travel frequently

Travel frequently to close (and sometimes far) destinations. You may get new ideas or new products to work upon.

If you want to become a super salesman, you need to travel and explore new places. Come out of your comfort zone by widening scope to excel new markets.

Travelling inherits you with opportunities that will definitely benefit you with abundance of knowledge. When you get a chance to meet new people, you are more inclined for possibilities of excelling your sales skills and business.

Wisdom

Way no. 423 to successful selling

Be patient regarding the deals

Patience in sales is as good as oxygen for life.
If you show impatience to customers, the customer doubts your product/service and assumes that you want to force sell by pressurizing.

Though the quality of your product/service is good, but due to impatient behavior it may affect your customers buying decision. So, it becomes highly important to maintain a balance between impatience and desire of closing the sale.

At the time of negotiation, your patience is tested. Your impatient conduct is a barrier in closing the deal.

Losing patience means losing sales

Way no. 424 to successful selling

How long to wait?

It is difficult to have a universal answer, but it's like testing your patience. It really depends on how hungry you are for sales and how promising the prospect is?

Generally speaking, waiting for half an hour is acceptable. But if you feel that the prospect is genuine, then waiting for 1-2 hours is also counted as fair period.

Remember, the more you wait for a genuine customer the more you are close to winning the sale. It shows that you are paying due respect to the customer and waiting till he is relatively free to attend you in person.

Greet them with enthusiasm, even if they see you after 2 hours. Don't let them realize your fatigue and exhaustion.

Waiting rewards

Way no. 425 to successful selling

Step in customers shoes

Step in customers shoes and see/feel for yourself in the situation.

This way, you will be more realistic and sincere in telling them your product/service and how they will be benefited from it.

Their worries and questions will be automatically answered by your inner self, and you can straight away start explaining them about your product/service without his questioning.

Analyze from the other side

Way no. 426 to successful selling

Your client database should include . . .

- Name
- Address
- City/state
- Landmark
- Zip code
- Phone numbers—home/office/mobile
- Email
- Website
- Date of birth/anniversary
- Past purchases
- Clients interest and budget
- Hobbies/passion
- Likes/dislikes
- Date of last call/meeting
- Proposed date of next call/meeting

Note: Not everyone is comfortable with sharing all the above details, but more the merrier.

Get complete info of your customer

Way no. 427 to successful selling

Find a KEY person who can give you customers

Building a new network of clients will take a lot of time, efforts and incur huge expenses. Instead, find a KEY person, who already has a network.

So, you need to search people among your existing circle, who have already established a good network and contacts, which they should be ready to share with you.

Customers will be comfortable to entertain you, as you are referred by someone whom they already know. You can always share your profit with them on successful sales which comes through their references.

Use networks for networking

Way no. 428 to successful selling

Activity and achievement are 2 different things

Many times people tend to draw same meaning of these 2 words—activity and achievement.

Activity is the process which brings achievement.

To add further, only being active will not bring achievement. A person can be active for 8 working hours, but what has he achieved in those 8 hours is what really matters in sales.

Example:
You travel for 4 hours for a single meeting and return with zero sales, and the next day you just walk around your neighborhood for 4 hours and bring 2 sales. In both the above cases you have been active for 4 hours, but only on second day you have achieved.

Work to achieve

Way no. 429 to successful selling

Do not say "NO" to any customer

Dont say "NO" to any customer.

If you are unable to give the client what they are looking for, then there is no way you can force-sale them your product/service.

In such situation, PLEASE refer someone you know who might fulfill their requirements.

People will remember you for helping them.

May be in future, these people reward you with some good orders or references, just as you did for them.

Help is always rewarded

Way no. 430 to successful selling

Common excuses

These are some common excuses unsuccessful salespeople love to give:

- I can't travel that long for this small order
- He/she is not worth visiting/talking
- I am sure he/she won't buy from me.
- That guy gets into my head.
- I could have sold more, if price of our product could have a bit lesser.
- This is not the right time to call/visit him/her
- He must have bought from competitor.
- Let's see tomorrow, not now.
- He/she had said 'NO' last time, he/she will not say 'YES" now.
- Its holiday, I should be enjoying and not taking any calls and appointments
- I am not confident
- I had explained him/her everything. Now I am waiting for him/her to call.
- I am sick / my xyz family member unwell.

Excuses = bad practice

Way no. 431 to successful selling

Keep clients updated on your achievements

It's important to keep your customers updated with your latest achievements to ensure that they know about your progress. This builds credibility and confidence for you and your company.

The following points could be shared with your customers:

- Your "Record Sales"
- New product/service
- New features added in existing product/service
- Awards won
- Expansions
- New ventures
- Media coverage
- Social participation

Bonding

Way no. 432 to successful selling

Move the prospect from 'No' to 'Know'

Most people say 'No' because they do not know enough about your product / services.

Every sales professional undergoes a particular product training before they can start approaching people for sales. Likewise every sales professional should understand and keep in mind that their customers are not trained on the product, hence you need to educate them with complete information and ensure they do not have any doubts/ confusions with regards to your product / services.

Make constant efforts to educate customers on your product / services as it will be always noticed and they do not hesitate to buy from you, as they now 'Know' and may say 'Yes' instead of saying 'No'.

Awareness is important

Referrals come from everywhere

Do not be under the impression that referrals come only from existing clients.
Referrals come from everywhere, and from every direction you possibly can imagine.

Expect referrals from all these:

- Existing clients
- Friends
- Neighbours
- Retailers around your home/office
- Your suppliers/vendors
- Government/educational institutions
- Professionals
- Media
- Various industries

Referrals save your time and money

Way no. 434 to successful selling

TWT and TWC

TWT = Total Working Time
TWC = Time With Customer

TWT and TWC is never equal, they cannot be matched. Generally, TWT can be of 8-10 hours for anyone. But do you spend all 10 hours with customer? The answer is NO.

We spend time in reading mails, replying, filing, sorting data, studying new products, meetings, updates, lunch & tea, planning holidays, and not to forget 'office gossips'.

To improve sales you need to improve on TWC. How much time you spend with a customer, maybe on phone, in meeting, handling his objections, sending him details, really matters.

The more the TWC the more are the sales.

TWC rewards

Way no. 435 to successful selling

Sacrifice a small margin, if the deal is really necessary

Be ready to sacrifice small amount of margin/profit, if the deal is really necessary.

Sometimes people like to bargain even for small amount, just to feel superior. By giving them what they want, make them feel proud and close the deal.

A small let-go will not affect your business in long run. May be the new customer recommends you a few friends or he buys more of your product/service later.

Small sacrifice will never matter in long run

Way no. 436 to successful selling

Price change during sales cycle

Sometimes price change happens when your deal is in process. This part needs to be handled smartly. Customers are very much likely to reject the new proposed price.

But be frank and straightforward to bring this to customers notice as soon as you come to know about it (even if it is not confirmed yet).

If you have even a slightest idea of price change at the time of proposing, then share it with your customer. It may help you in prompt closing and full advance payment.

Note: If you have received the token amount of the order before price change, then it's wise to abide with the primary proposal price, or you lose the deal.

Be careful with price changes

Way no. 437 to successful selling

Be with customers virtually

Make your presence felt in customers mind, wherever they are.

Giving a impactful presentation of your product/service will ensure that they visualize it many times.

Relate use of your product/service in customers daily routine (how it would help him/her simplify his/her work with ease). And when a person thinks about something very often he tends to buy it.

Sometimes, giving away a sample helps a lot in this process.

Be in customers mind

Way no. 438 to successful selling

When your presentations go wrong

We all are human beings; we do make mistakes and do go wrong sometimes. If your demonstration goes muddled, please do not panic, it happens with everyone atleast once in entire career.

You need not get embarrassed and should take it playfully. Accept it and try to cover it with some humour.

Example:
If your presentation is having some starting problems, you can crack a joke—"it seems it won't start until I get a big order from you guys"

If you happen to drop snacks on floor and make a mess, then you can remark—"I thought the carpet was hungry".

Handle it anyway

Way no. 439 to successful selling

Always agree with customer

Even if the customer is wrong, always agree with them by saying "right sir", "rightly said", etc.

Because if you do not agree with them, it will break the sales process and they will turn away without buying your product or service. So you better be with him.

Try to please every customer and ask him what more information he requires to get the deal done.

Never disagree

Way no. 440 to successful selling

Let everyone know what you do

Talk about your product/service with everyone you meet (in brief and please do not start your demo/presentation instantly). Let people around you know what you do. Let them grow curious and come to you for more inputs. You never know who is willing to do business with you?

This list should not only include people you meet in parties, weddings, etc., but also the following:

- Teachers of your children
- Gym instructor
- Gardener
- Gate keeper
- Laundry person
- Housekeeper/maid
- Electrician
- Person sitting next to you in bus/train/flight
- Newspaper vendor
- And every person you can think of . . . .

Get famous around your address

Way no. 441 to successful selling

You cannot sell to all

No sales person in history has ever achieved 100% sales with all prospects they met.

The probability is between 5% to 8% only.

If you meet/call 100 customers, around 50 % will show interest in hearing/meeting you. Out of that 50%, only 25% will actually show interest in buying. And eventually, 5%-8% will actually buy from your original customer list.

So, to make 5-8 sales, you probably need to have a customer base of around 100 people.

Not all are buyers

Way no. 442 to successful selling

Existing customers

Apart from making new customers, it's really necessary to hold on to old/current customers. This database is important for your future sales, in terms of repeated orders, referrals, new launches, faith, trust, branding, etc.

You may lose a customer if:

- You do not attend his complain
- You promise and do not deliver
- Your product didn't serve their purpose
- Your product is of poor quality
- Your competitor wooed them
- You have lost rapport/trust
- You contact them only for selling
- They have moved away
- Decision maker has changed

Do not forget existing customers

Way no. 443 to successful selling

When people say 'It's too costly'

When people say that your product/service is too costly, it does not mean it is the price that is holding them from buying. The reality is very different.

In reality, they are suppressing their decision on the basis of the following points:

- They do not actually want to buy
- They already have bought it from others
- Someone offering cheaper than you
- They cannot afford it
- It's not fitting their budget
- They are expecting discounts

Nothing is too costly

Way no. 444 to successful selling

How to reach a difficult prospect

At times we come across some prospects that are difficult to approach. Either they are very busy or have gatekeepers (secretary, managers, etc.) who screen their schedule.

The easy way to get these people is to make good contact with their gatekeepers. Send them email, faxes, etc. for your introduction. Then call for confirmation of the receipt, and ask for appointment.

Other way is to directly walk in the office after office hours; you may find the actual prospect. Because, such people do stay a bit late in office and have no one to screen their visitors at that time. You may not succeed in first approach, but trying for 3-4 times will surely help to meet these prospects.

Try hard, you will succeed

Way no. 445 to successful selling

Quotations

Quotations represent general information of a particular product / services, with its pricing.

It is prepared in common and not made as per any individual's preference. It can be obtained by all, without any bargains.

When you issue quotations, also inform your customers about the added benefits, they will enjoy on booking your product / service. Do not forget to mention the limitation of the added benefits that you promised to your customer. Routine yourself of giving quotations to your customer as this activity will bring you closer to the actual sale.

Keep buffer for negotiation

Way no. 446 to successful selling

Always remember the old 80:20 rule, it still works

80 % of your results come from 20% of your activity.

Learn which 20% is that, which will bring you most of the results.

Note that in any bank, only 20% of account holder's count for 80% of banks' business. Similarly, you need to narrow down your search on those 20% of prospective customers amongst your database. Focusing on these 20% customers also benefits you in saving your precious time and resources.

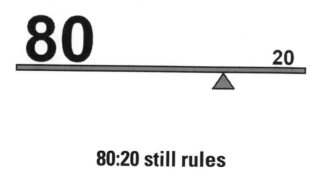

80:20 still rules

Way no. 447 to successful selling

Immediately apply whatever you have learnt new

Whatever you have learnt new, it may be through some course, from people, new trends, mistakes or new product, etc. act on it immediately.

Just learning and keeping it in mind or writing it in your idea bank book will not help you, you need to act on it ASAP.

Remember if you do not put your new ideas in action, someone else will master the skill and you will regret later for losing your business.

Implement

Way no. 448 to successful selling

Don't leave before asking for next appointment

When you meet your customer for the first time, you cannot expect them to buy your product / service instantly. Your customer needs time to make his decision due to several aspects like family discussion, product study, urgency etc.

A successful sales person understands such situations and makes a constant effort to meet them at regular intervals, asking for next appointments till the time he / she gets a final answer from his customer.

Confirming their next appointment brings him / her closer to sale.

Appointments . . . sales!

Way no. 449 to successful selling

You are accountable for everything

Since a sales professional usually interacts and comes in contact with the outsiders, his presence denotes the face of the product and company. A sales person is accountable for everything involved in sales.

One needs to understand and be responsible enough to ensure and maintain credibility of the company and its product / services.

Take responsibility

Way no. 450 to successful selling

Umbrella questions

These are very small and simple questions you ask your customers to make them speak. By asking these questions you get to know more about what they are looking for. These also help us to get additional information from them.

Examples of some umbrella questions:

- Why sir/mam?
- Can you elaborate it please?
- Any other examples you could share?
- Could I be of any more help?

Note: when you are not sure what to ask, try using these words in your sentences—*how, where, when, what, how* and *why,* etc.,

Ignite them to speak

Way no. 451 to successful selling

Do not put limitations on your ideas

Others are not the cause of your limited thinking it's you who impose limitations on yourself.

Explore to new heights; do not limit yourself from exploring new ideas which can be implemented in addition to your sales strategies.

Sometimes a small idea can change your sales business drastically.

Do not let others set your limitations.

Ideas = reward

Way no. 452 to successful selling

Open / close ended questions

Open ended questions are subject to explanatory answers. A reply to an open ended question may be a lengthy suggestion or explanation that does not end in a single Yes or No.

What, When, Where, Why etc are all open ended questions.

Close ended questions mean the exact opposite, where the customer has only 2 choices to answer either Yes or No. It limits the opposite person from anything they wish to say.

- Are you happy?
- May I take this?
- Can we go?

Are all examples of close ended questions.

Question wisely

Way no. 453 to successful selling

There are always some common objections

Customers always have some common objections in regards to product / service. It is advisable to note such objections and be prepared with the answers well in advance.

As a good sales-man answers all the objections in advance, which may arise later. Learn to disarm objections before they arise.

Your presentation / demo should be explanatory enough that customers get all their objections / doubts cleared in one go.

Kindly answer objections

Way no. 454 to successful selling

Hire cautiously, but fire immediately

While choosing the right team players, you should not start appointing candidates like buying day to day's grocery. Study their profile well, talk to their references, verify their qualification and whatever they have mentioned in their resume.

In the reverse case, i.e., while asking someone to leave your company, you need not wait for long. Even if you have signed contract of 1 month notice from either parties. You release one months' salary / share / commission and stop the employee from all involvements immidietly. Because if he/she stays in company for one month, he will spoil the other people around him and will destroy the decorum of your company.

Note: this is very necessary to protect the interest of other salespeople around.

Sometimes, being rude saves business

Way no. 455 to successful selling

Do not spend too much time with a customer

Do not spend too much of your time with a customer whom you like or have many things in common, because every single customer has a limited potential to buy.

Even if you end up spending extra time, he is not going to buy anything extra from you.

You need to be wise enough to take best possible advantage from every customer you meet in considerable time frame.

Perfect usage of time

Way no. 456 to successful selling

Never assume clients reactions

It is always better to get a clear understanding on what your customer means. Do not assume anything, as this will create confusions and complications later.

Examples:

- In a grocery shop, you sell mugs in dozens. A customer approaches you for 6 pieces, and without confirming you assume as 6 dozens.
- Pearl white color is very much in demand in cars, and you assume that every customer will like the same, and you do not keep other colors on display.

Assumptions are unhealthy

Way no. 457 to successful selling

Respect Law

Selling is not only a matter of deal between 2 people, but it is transfer of ownership in most of the cases.

Do respect all the regional laws attached to your product / service.

Never venture unethical ways to get a deal done; otherwise you will spend more time and money to fight the cases in court, than the profit you made in the deal.

But, if the customer is holding you responsible for no good and valid reasons, then do approach consumer court or similar authorities to protect your name and brand.

Laws and bylaw

Way no. 458 to successful selling

Be alone for 2-3 hours in a week

One should practice to keep everything aside for 2-3 hours in a week and think about growing business.

It is necessary because, every day we are answering many calls, visiting customers, coordinating with distributors, etc. But being alone for 2-3 hours will give you essential time required for perfect planning.

Following things should be considered when you want to make business plans staying alone:

- Put DO NOT DISTURB tag
- Keep away your phones
- Do self-talks
- Write down the points ASAP
- Avoid distractions
- Keep walking

Be on your own

Way no. 459 to successful selling

Pricing of your product / services

You have to be very cautious while considering price for your products / services. Pricing should not be changed often and you have to consider the following factors before applying a price tag:

- Market survey
- Forecasting
- Competitors
- Demand and supply
- Additional features
- Upcoming products / services
- Economic conditions
- Customers feed back
- Manufacturing and maintaining expenses
- Profits in the long run
- Breakeven point
- Customization as per special requirements

Price wisely

Way no. 460 to successful selling

Discount or Extra?

The better way to explain, what I mean is to start with an example here.

Example: If you are a sales person from some energy drinks / beverage company. Your selling price is $100.00 per 1000 ml, and you wish to do a promotional activity for increasing sales. Study the difference in 2 offers:

Offer 1: Get 50% extra
i.e. 1500 ml in $ 100 = $ 0.15 per ml

Offer 2: Get 50% off.
i.e. 1000 ml in $ 50 = $ 0.20 per ml

So please, do double check before offering any discounts / schemes. In the above case, though both the offers seem similar, but offer 1 will earn you more profits.

Promotional offer

Way no. 461 to successful selling

Optimism and realism

All sales persons are optimistic by nature; this is what makes them successful. But over-optimism can ruin sales.

Everyone gets annoyed with people who show over-optimism, which really sounds fake. Such people are not believed upon and remain non-achievers.

Make sure not to pull out unrealistic figures under over-optimism. The figures should be achievable in actual.

A successful sales person has to be **realistically optimistic**, which means a proper combination of optimism with realism.

Consider realism prior to optimism

Way no. 462 to successful selling

Smart buyers rely on customer reviews

It is true that buyers have become smarter than they were 2-3 decades back. Smart buyers rely on customer's reviews the product / service prior to making any buying decision.

They read blogs, comments, star ratings, etc on internet or weekly magazines. More than 50% of people rely on such information.

So make sure your product/service has good ratings and is full of great experiences from your customers.

The more you keep your customers happy, the more good they will share with media.

Maintain your rapport

Way no. 463 to successful selling

Recognize your weaknesses

Your smallest weakness can prove fatal for sales. To recognize your weak area, talk to your mentors, seniors, colleagues. In some cases a customer can be the best medium to point out your weakness.

To overcome your weaknesses, practice:

- Writing it with its solution
- Reading / watching self improvement articles
- Meditation
- Learning from someone similar
- Analyzing your past

Note: A proven method, if you practice something for more than 21 days, it becomes a routine.

Win over weaknesses

Way no. 464 to successful selling

The power of persuasion

Persuasion is the process which changes peoples' beliefs or attitudes with logical reasoning.

A sales person should try to convince and influence the customers to adopt his/her ideas, objectives, etc., as a strategy for selling the products / services.

It's necessary to learn persuasion to make good sales. Persuasion does not mean arguments or hard selling. It's convincing people in a right way.

Understand other persons needs properly and give them enough time for clearing all their objections and doubts.

Convince them the benefits and usages of your products / services over your competitors'.

Persuade

Way no. 465 to successful selling

Everyone gets 24 hours a day

Make good use of time in doing better activities, upgrading skills, learning new things, etc.

Successful sales people don't get extra hours, they too managed with 24 hours a day only but they find ways to utilize those 24 hours more wisely and productively.

Simple division of hours—10 hours work, 8 hours sleep, 4 hours family 2 hours investing in yourself (reading, learning, studying, making strategies, discussions, etc)

Mismanagement of time is the biggest cause of failure.

Do not mismanage time

Way no. 466 to successful selling

Pillar

Just like a building, a particular product / service is in existence or standing because of people associated with it and can be considered as pillars of the company.

You have to get yourself noticed as one of the strong pillars' in the success of your product / service.

When a sales professional takes a pride on being one of the pillars, they open opportunities of wisdom and a promising career.

Create a heavy importance of yourself, in such a way that survival of the organization becomes challenging without you.

Be nucleus of your company

Way no. 467 to successful selling

Formal & casual wear

Formals on weekends are fine sometimes, but casuals on weekdays are very important.

Many times it all depends on customer to customer. If you are going to meet an existing customer, it won't matter what you wear.
But if you are meeting a new face, even on weekend, go in formals.

What if you are on the way to meet existing customer in casuals and you get a call from a prospective customer to meet immediately or in next 1-2 hours?

It is wise to be in formals all the times. If you wear casuals, customers take you casually.

Wear professionalism

Way no. 468 to successful selling

Selling is not talking

This is the biggest misconception, most of the new sales people have. They think that just being a good talker (conversationalist) is sufficient and only qualification required for closing sales.

Though being extrovert is necessary in sales, but there are many other factors that are obligatory.

Please keep in mind that it is just not about closing sales, it is about opening new relations. You are out there to make a customer and not a sale.

Note: Listening to you and doing business with you are two different aspects.

Qualify yourself

Way no. 469 to successful selling

Remember, you are dependent on customer

Remember, you are dependent on customer, and vice versa. You need business from them to run your company / home. So, treat them like GOD.

- Avoid not arguing with them.
- Call them at their convenience, not yours.
- Your false promises will divert them to your competitor.
- They are your business partner.
- They expect courtesy.
- You have to help them with their needs.
- They are just other human beings whom you approach for their benefits.

You depend on customer

Way no. 470 to successful selling

Trust your product/service

The most primary step you need to develop is trust in your product / service. Your customers will never buy from you until you seem to be confident on your product or service.

To develop a trust in your products / services you need to:

- Gain knowledge
- Learn its features and benefits
- Others involvement in making the product
- Comparison with competitors
- Make sure it fulfills customers requirements
- Understand product / service value
- Experience it personaly
- Eliminate drawbacks, if any

Conviction

Way no. 471 to successful selling

Most customers do not complain

It has been observed that most customers find it easy to change the vendor / supplier instead of complaining over small issues. Products / services of lower range do not excite customer to waste time in complaining. Example: soaps, tea bags, pens, bed sheets, cookies, etc. This leaves the sales person / manufacturer without any sort of feedback.

The best and easy way to gather information on customer's reaction is to keep a survey book at the outlets. Make it easily visible and accessible. You can even appoint representative at the outlets to take direct feedback.

Note: do not force customers to enter their contact numbers, as many are not comfortable with this. You just concentrate in getting genuine feedback and suggestions.

Step out

Way no. 472 to successful selling

Give sufficient time to decide

Time taken in making a buying decision varies from product to product and customer to customer.

Non-expensive and routine products doesn't really require more time for decision making.
But expensive purchases like properties, cars, holiday packages, etc will definitely require fair amount of time.

You need to be patient with such deals.

You may have to explain the whole product/service more than once, and wait for the closing.

Do not force customer to close the deal even if it takes a bit more than the usual time.

Be patient

Way no. 473 to successful selling

Leave a good impression everywhere you go

Remember, if a customer has a bad experience with you, he/she will talk about it with as many as 10 people. But, on the other hand, if he/she had a good experience, he/she will probably talk to only 4 people.

Its human psychology to spread negative news / experience faster than sharing positive news / experience.

Example:

If a company is going bankrupt, all media covers it instantly. But when the company is doing good business and making profits, hardly any media covers it.

So, make sure, people talk good about you.
It is really very difficult to build the brand again, if its lost.

Be impressive

Way no. 474 to successful selling

Variety of customers

Understanding the type of customers will make your selling easy. These are:

<u>Relationship buyers:</u> These are customers who give high importance to relationship. Show your readiness for good future relations.

<u>Impatience buyers:</u> These are ready buyers and do not wish to wait for purchase of the product / service. They already have knowledge and have done research.

<u>Puzzled buyers:</u> These customers are not sure if they really need your product / service or not. They are confused. You need to educate these customers on the features and benefit of your product / service.

<u>Vigilant buyers:</u> These customer want every detail of your product / service. They are always extra cautious while purchasing anything.

Customers vary

Way no. 475 to successful selling

Keep your daily records

Keeping your daily records is essential to keep track of your growth.

It should basically include:

- Number of calls made
- Number of appointments fixed
- Number of meetings done
- Number of sales done
- Number of bad calls/meetings
- Why customer said Yes / No?
- Number of referrals you got and followed
- Next time/day of calling/meeting the customer
- Average time spent with clients
- Number of deals you need to crack

Write down all significant points daily

Way no. 476 to successful selling

If you are selling through website, then . . .

If you are doing web based sales, then you need to be very quick in responding to orders, as order keep coming round the clock.

Remember, your customers do not have to go out and shop, that's why they have thought of using your web based service. So, they expect fast service. You need to reply them as soon as possible, and send them expected date of delivery.

Be clear with packaging/delivery charges, if any.

Send them proper payment receipt, if they have made the payment through net banking.

Selling on web is 24 hours business

Way no. 477 to successful selling

Have some daily targets

You have to have some daily targets. So that each morning you have something to start the day with and which is going to help you a lot in your business.

Break your yearly/monthly targets into daily targets.

If you need to make 100 sales every month then you need to make 4 sales daily, if you work 25 days a month, and for 4 sales you may need to meet 20 people daily.

Then, if you meet only 15 people someday due to unavoidable circumstances, you need to catch up with extra 5 people the very next day. Or your targets will differ at the end of the month, resulting in loss of business.

Utilize each day of yours in improving your business.

Break monthly / yearly targets into daily targets

Way no. 478 to successful selling

Sales burn-out

Situations may arise, even after trying hard and using all your skills you do not get expected results, this stage is known as sales burnout.

Few indicators of 'Sales burnout' are:

- Self doubt
- Time consuming approval process
- Lack of proper sleep
- Impatience
- Constantly worried and fantasizing
- Lying
- Impulsive decision
- Lack of creativity
- Procrastination
- Loneliness
- Being unwell regularly

Kick burnouts

Way no. 479 to successful selling

Hot buttons

Every individual in this world has his own preferences in choosing a particular product / service and penchant of benefits. A smart sales professional is always on pursuit for that weak point of his customer and on detecting the same; they make their move by emphasizing on the weakest buying point of that buyer.

Example:

When a customer arrives with his family to buy a car, and then you notice that your customer and his family are really impressed by the 'sunroof' feature in your car, you must instantly understand that the particular feature is the Hot button you need to use wisely.

Hunt and play

Way no. 480 to successful selling

Practice new strategies on low probability customer

Whenever you want to introduce new strategies or methods to increase sales, ensure you try the same, with a low probability customer so that even if you fail, it does not bring you a huge loss.

New strategies do not guarantee confirmed results and involve risk.

Example:

A sales person from garment industry, who wish to introduce his latest trendy shirt, should ensure that he tries to sell it to someone who will not bad mouth or affect his credibility in market like a close friend, relative etc. On the contrary if he tries to sell the shirt to a new high profile customer, there are chances of getting marked down, losing potential business, and may also lead to unsatisfied customer.

New strategies needs careful application

Way no. 481 to successful selling

Become a sales doctor

Just as a doctor diagnoses the problem of patient before giving any medicine, you study the customer first. What are their needs, what are they expecting from you and your product/service.

Listen to them carefully and probe tactfully, By doing so, you get chance to provide the best suitable solution.

You need to understand that every customer is different and their priorities differ. Hence applying your strategies appropriately is a must. Because, what sales strategies worked on one person, the same will not necessarily work on others.

Sales doctor

Way no. 482 to successful selling

Customers' view

While explaining your product / services or during your presentations, always remember that you discuss least in terms of numbers or figures to your customers.

It is a natural phenomenon that we tend to visualize benefits derived from a particular product / service and not its price tag. The moment we think of a price tag our brain gets conscious to think about commercials and overlook benefits of the products / services benefits.

Example:

While selling a holiday package to your customer, when you constantly discuss about the destination and sightseeing ... your customer tends to feel himself with his family at the chosen location. The moment you mention a 'Number (price tag)' your customer sees it as a warning.

Visualize product and benefits

Way no. 483 to successful selling

Where to find new customers?

You will find new customers from:

- Referrals
- Local newspapers
- Visiting cards you exchanged
- Friends/relatives
- Newly moved companies/peoples
- Old enquiries
- Unsatisfied customers of your competitors
- Newly married / arrival of new family members in neighborhood
- Trade directories
- Trade fairs
- Common place where people usually gather
- Competitor moving out of business/location

Become radar to catch all signals of new customers

Way no. 484 to successful selling

Buyer and consumer

You have to identify needs of buyers as well as consumers while selling your product / service.

Buyers are people who buy for consumers. They may not be the actual end-users. They buy out of necessity.

Consumers are the ones, who are often called as end-users, they do not transfer or sell the product / service to another person. They buy systematically, and are the actual users.

Example:
A florist has to consider distributors and individuals. Distributors buy according to their retailers' demand or the venue where the flowers are to be sent (hotels, stage, weddings, parties, etc.), where as individuals buy for themselves during special occasions (festivals, anniversaries, etc.)

Consider both

Way no. 485 to successful selling

Do a little more than you are supposed to do

Always do more than what you are supposed to do. It means that always put an extra effort than needed.

Give people something extra, and you will get something extra too.
As the old saying goes—to get something you need to first give something. So to get more, give more.

This little 'more' can be in the form of some information, guidance, help, recommendations, etc. or even going an extra mile to drop someone rather than asking him to get down and walk from where you wanted to go.

These little MORE's will not cost you anything, but when people get these without asking for, you make and create a bonding with them.

Do more to get more

Way no. 486 to successful selling

Do not get frustrated

You will certainly come across people who love to check your patience by asking too many questions or irritating and repeated questions.

Just keep calm, it's their habit. Chances of closing the deals with such people are 50:50.

Either they are seriously interested in buying from you, thats why they are asking too many questions or they are just wasting your time.

Learn to do a trial close after answering a few questions. Taking out the order form for confirming order will help you a lot in such situations.

Use tactics

Way no. 487 to successful selling

Cracking competitors' clientele

Many competitors will find this unethical, but this point has to be covered.

What do you do if a customer says, he is happy with his 5 year old supplier, and doesn't even want to think on replacing them?

You can give your samples for free, if they find yours of superior quality, they may rethink on it.

Or, you can leave your details and ask them to call you whenever there is a shortage or delay of supply from their current vendor. If you make it on time, you just got the gate pass.

Create opportunity

Way no. 488 to successful selling

Meet 5 new faces everyday

The most important aspect of sales professional is to encounter atleast 5 new faces every day, as this helps you in exploring potential opportunities. It is essential in order to generate large number of prospects.

Meeting 5 people per day will expand your prospect strength by more than 1800 people a year. Considering a consistent effort in the mentioned manner you will have a strong network of more than 9,000 people associated with you in 5 years. These 5 new faces may introduce you to more references, who may also bring you business.

More people more business

Way no. 489 to successful selling

Give discount only when required

Do not ever give discount beforehand. This will lower the value of your product/service.

This should come into discussion only when you are sure that the prospect is actually going to take decision of buying and he is now negotiating for the product/service.

Discounts should be the last resort to cement the sale. Try to barter your discount with some benefit to you and your company.

Example 1—Instead of regular 10% of booking amount, take 50% and give appropriate discount.

Example 2—instead of 1 unit, ask to buy 2 or more units and give discount accordingly.

Customers usually tend to gain the best out of every product/services and sacrificing a small margin will merely affect in your profits.

Do not drive sales by discounts

Way no. 490 to successful selling

Extroverts find it easy to sell

Extroverts find it very easy to deal with unknown people. They are crowd pullers, and grab attention of everyone easily.

They gel up with almost every person, and start their selling mission smartly.

Such people are expert in the ability to connect with strangers & take up discussions which ultimately lead to their product/ services. They smartly create a curiosity/ need in the other persons mind making them a prospect.

Extroverts are majorly noticed in social gathering, exhibitions, social websites etc.

Become an extrovert

Way no. 491 to successful selling

Only aim, do not blame

All of us have a negative judgment of what should or should not have been happened?

Since no one can change the past, looking at the past and blaming others is not as productive as looking at the future.

Successful people refer to experiences from experts and consider a positive approach in solving problems.

Aiming for solutions is always worth rather than playing the blame game.

By blaming others you are limiting your growth. Instead learn from others mistake and excel in life.

Do not play blame game

Way no. 492 to successful selling

Visualize your sales

Draw a mental picture of your successful sales. It will create a positive impact on sales.

Unless you dream of something; how can you achieve it?

Famous inventor Thomas Alva Edison also drew a mental picture of an electric bulb in his mind before inventing it. Would that have been possible without creating a mental picture? The answer is NO.

Everything is created two times. Once in your mind and second time in reality. Create a blue print in your mind of what you wish to achieve, just like what the architects do.

So, to achieve good sales, think as if you have already achieved it, and naturally, you tend to achieve what you think for the whole day.

Create pictures in mind

Way no. 493 to successful selling

What does "O" mean to you?

How do you look at this particular letter "O"?

It may be an English alphabet "O" for a few and "zero" for a few.

Take this "O" for <u>O</u>pportunities and not for <u>O</u>bstacles.

If you see "O" for Obstacles, you are going to get many in your way, and if you see "O" for Opportunities, then, you can expect many in your way.

And if you see it as a Zero, you will get these too.

'O' = opportunities

Way no. 494 to successful selling

Do take calls at odd times

Picking up calls at odd hours means good business, not immidietly but certainly in near future.

People calling at odd hours, means they are in urgent need of your product/service, and they have preferred you over your competitors. Hear them. They get a good impression of yours when you show willingness in helping them at these hours. They can mean a serious business.

They feel honored, when you attend them even after your working hours.

This will always be remembered by the customer. And they will appreciate you.

Others' urgency = your business

Way no. 495 to successful selling

Use these words in discussions

Addition	Important	Precious
Advantage	Improved	Proceeds
Benefit	Income	Productive
Best	Increase	Progress
Development	Loved	Proven
Done	Monetary	Quality
Dynamic	More	Remarkable
Excellent	Most	Reserved
First	Motivate	Safe
Genuine	Opportunity	Saves
Goal	Outstanding	Suitable
Great	Perfect	Sure
Growing	Positive	Thanks
Helpful	Possible	Value
Higher	Powerful	Worth

Remember all these words

Way no. 496 to successful selling

Do not be afraid of rejections

Majority of sales professionals end up making mistakes in fear of rejection. Rejection should always be taken positively as it gives you a chance to sharpen your skills & advance your expertise in your field of business.

Successful sales professionals are never discouraged by rejections & deal the same by taking it as an advantage in the following manner:

- Do not take rejections personaly
- Make a list of common reasons of rejection.
- Question yourself—why did a particular customer rejected the proposal? And you get the answer.
- Approach the customer with various solutions.
- Bring a positive change for future prospects.
- Add value to the product/Services.

Rejection = Opportunity

Way no. 497 to successful selling

Once a customer, always a customer

"Once a customer, always a customer" is the fine old technique to cherish your business in optimum manner.

The term proves absolutely right and should be practiced thoroughly by every sales person as it saves your precious time and other recourses which are required in finding altogether a new customer.

You need to adhere to the following points to win the customer repeatedly:

- Best service.
- Maintain same enthusiasm as your first sale.
- Keep up with your commitments.
- Maintaining transparency.
- Doing a little more than you are supposed to do.
- Promising less and delivering more.

Same customer = easy business

Way no. 498 to successful selling

Use "Limited Offer" tool

"Limited offer" works wonders. This tool creates urgency on taking decision to buy, and makes customers act fast.

Use this tool for quick sales. People tend to buy under such schemes, as they think they are amongst the lucky few who get such offer. It helps sales persons to promote new product/services in bulk sales. Giving discounts, add-ons, etc is also possible because of huge sales.

Limited offer help in :

- Future sales
- Negotiating with retailers/distributors
- Brand building
- Instant profits
- Product stability
- Business promotion
- Cost efficiency

Make them feel lucky

Way no. 499 to successful selling

Input = output

It's simple and self explanatory, to get 100% results you need to work 100%.

Your input in your presentation, preparedness, product knowledge, appearance, punctuality, manners, etc will decide your sales output.

If your input is all these 500 ways then your success in selling is guaranteed.

You have graduated in successful selling . . . . happy sales

Way no. 500 to successful selling

Amongst the hundreds of books I read, would like to suggest a few, which really inspired me:

- Law of success—Napoleon Hill
- The one minute millionaire—Mark Victor Hansen & Robert G. Allen
- The monk who sold his Ferrari—Robin Sharma
- The science of getting rich—Wallace D. Wattles
- The 21 secrets of self-made millionaires—Brian Tracy
- Grow rich while you sleep—Ben Sweetland
- The secret—Rhonda Byrne
- The Aladdin factor—Jack Canfield & Mark Hansen
- The magic of thinking big—David J. Schwartz
- The alchemist—Paulo Coelho
- The one minute manager—Ken Blanchard & Spencer Johnson
- Body language—Allan & Barbara Pease
- The power of confidence—Norman Vincent Peale
- The power of positive thinking—Norman Vincent Peale
- Cash flow quadrants—Robert T. Kiyosaki
- Rich dad poor dad—Robert T. Kiyosaki
- The magic of believing—Claude M. Bristol
- Tuesdays with morrie—Mitch Albom
- The decision book—Mikael Krogerus & Roman Tschappeler
- Who moved my cheese?—Dr. Spencer Johnson
- How to win friends influence People—Dale Carnegie
- The intelligent investor—Benjamin Graham

Thank you and God bless you all.